The Activist Angler

The Activist Angler

STEPHEN DUNCOMBE

With drawings by
Elle Azul Duncombe-Mills

OR Books
New York · London

Published by OR Books, New York and London
Visit our website at www.orbooks.com

All rights information: rights@orbooks.com

First printing 2023

Library of Congress Cataloging-in-Publication Data: A catalog record for this book is available from the Library of Congress.
British Library Cataloging in Publication Data: A catalog record for this book is available from the British Library.

Typeset by Lapiz Digital.

paperback ISBN 978-1-68219-501-7 • ebook ISBN 978-1-68219-411-9

To Michael Young

1975–2021

Gone Fishin'

Contents

Activist Angler

For everything there is a season. Out on Cape Cod, where I do much of my fishing, the legal season varies from fish to fish and whether you are fishing in fresh or saltwater, but practically the fishing season lasts from early spring to late fall. My activism has seasons too, albeit on longer cycles. Every ten years or so I step back from day-to-day community building and troublemaking and take a breather. From my late teens to late twenties, I was a campus activist, then ramped down to finish my dissertation and concentrate on my first teaching job. Over the next decade, I worked as a community organizer in the Lower East Side before putting activism on the back burner again to raise a family and write a book about creative forms of activism. As our children got older, I took up activism once more, this time as a trainer of artist-activists around the globe. After ten years as co-director of the Center for Artistic Activism, I decided it was time for another break. The Center was in good hands, the world of activism was doing just fine without a middle-aged white man like me front and center, and the COVID crises had forced me, my family, and the rest of the world into a state of quarantine. So, I took up fishing.

When I was young I loved to go fishing. My mother would drop me off at a local reservoir or brackish estuary in the coastal New England town where I grew up, and for hours I would cast my lures out into the water, waiting for a strike from a slippery eel or toothy snapper blue, but mostly relaxing into the rhythm of casting and retrieving. As a teenager, punk rock, skateboarding, and sex seemed far more attractive than being covered with fish scales, so I stopped fishing. When I got older, other things took the place of guitars and skateboards and teenage dalliances, yet I didn't return to fishing for nearly four decades. The pandemic seemed like the perfect time to pick up rod and reel again. I needed a break from the stress of living during an unmanaged pandemic, I wanted time and space away from people where I didn't have to worry about wearing a mask or getting too close, and I needed an escape from the burdens of being an activist at what felt like a time of political apocalypse. So, I went fishing. Every day. Sometimes multiple times a day. Blissfully isolated on the tip of Cape Cod, I'd fish for large and small mouth bass in the kettle ponds in the early mornings. At midday I'd cast off the harbor jetty as the young striper "schoolies" made the run from estuary to bay as the tides turned, and then fish the ocean beaches for striped bass and bluefish as the sun went down.

After forty years, I had to reteach myself how to fish, and so I approached the practice with what Zen masters call Beginner's Mind. With no habits or tradition to fall back upon, every fish successfully caught or line hopelessly snarled provided a clear lesson. With hours spent doing little more than casting and retrieving — catching fish being a fraction of the time spent fishing — I had a lot of time to think about these lessons I was learning. One of the things I thought about a lot was activism. Even on my political hiatus, I was still consulting on activist projects, and as I gave advice on a global campaign for free COVID vaccines, or an art project aimed at reintegrating formerly incarcerated people back into their communities, or using artistic activism as a way to fight corruption in the Western Balkans and West Africa, I found myself drawing from my fishing experiences. Fishing, I discovered, has a lot to teach about the art of activism and, perhaps even more, about staying active as an activist.

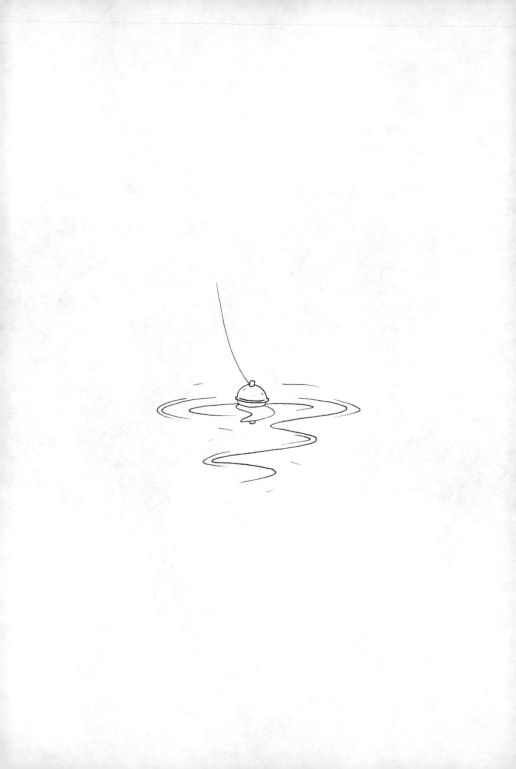

Practicing Patience

To be a good angler you need patience. In fact, in order to not quit the first day out when you realize just how eventless it can be, you need patience. Fishing is often frustratingly unproductive. The name itself says it all: most of the time when you are fishing, you are not actually catching, you are just fishing. Fishing is also repetitive. You cast out and you reel in, hoping there's a fish nearby and it likes what you have to offer. Cast out and reel in. Cast out and reel in. Cast out and reel in. I quickly learned that to enjoy fishing I needed to embrace the process and not just be in it for the product. That's not to say that the product, catching a fish, doesn't matter — it does — it's just that arriving at the moment when a fish is on your line may take a long, long time. But with enough patience, the moment will come: the fish will be biting, one will grab hold of your offering, you'll feel the tug, your rod will bend, and you will experience the heart-pounding thrill of catching a fish, and perhaps even the pleasure of eating one too. But without practicing patience, none of this will happen.

I remember once asking Dread Scott, a committed activist-artist who, like me, was approaching middle age, how he kept the faith that his work was going to have an impact. He responded with a personal metaphor. "I like cycling," he said, "and if you're a great bike rider and you're riding in the Tour de France, and you happen to be riding in the seven years that Lance Armstrong is riding, you're probably not going to win. Even if you're a great cyclist. It's just the balance of things don't work in your favor." For most of my activist life, the balance of things have not been in my favor. For nearly forty years I have been going to meetings and planning actions. I work with amazing people on righteous causes, but those with more money and power usually win. Yet I, and countless other activists, keep doing the seemingly unproductive and repetitive labor of activism. Why? Because, as Dread went on to explain, it's about waiting for what happens in that eighth year: when Lance Armstrong is not in the Tour de France (or, as it turns out, gets banned from cycling for cheating). There are moments when the balance of things is in our favor, when historical alignments are in the right position, and we do win. Then the world changes, even if only a little. Waiting for those moments takes patience, and when they come you need to have kept up your training.

Time Alone

I started fishing again to be alone. The immediate impetus was the COVID crisis, when social distancing became the norm and being alone at water's edge was one of the few places I didn't need to worry about wearing a mask, but I came to enjoy the solitude for other reasons. As an activist, teacher, and parent, there are always meetings to attend, classes to teach, emails to respond to, and sibling fights to referee. It's a continuous conversation. Which is why I enjoy the silence of fishing. Fish don't talk, and they don't want to be spoken to. (Although I do usually say a few words to them before I release them.) In this silence, I listen to the other sounds around me: the lap of the water, the scurrying of an unseen animal in the brush, the laugh of seagulls or honking of ducks, the truck downshifting as it makes the climb up the rise on nearby Route 6. Against this natural white noise, and with my physical movements engaged in the regular rhythms of casting and retrieving, my mind wanders: going to spaces and stopping at places it's usually too busy to go, or going nowhere, simply resting, before I go back into the world.

Activism and organizing are collective activities. Social change does not happen because of a Great Leader doing a Great Act, it happens because lots of people, working together, do lots of things over and over, collecting more and more people with them as they go. This collective activity is exciting, but it can also be exhausting, especially for someone who is a bit of an introvert like myself. When planning for an action or working in a social movement, with every spare minute spent meeting or talking or strategizing with someone, it's really easy to get sucked into constant socializing. Then there are those times in history when the world explodes, and you are out on the street marching and protesting with masses of people every day, and every day becomes a group experience. All this collective activity is necessary for movement building, but in my four decades of activism I have seen many, many activists get so caught up in the movement (and urged by their comrades to do so) that they forget to make time to be by themselves. They forget to take care of themselves. As a result they burn out, and eventually, inevitably, they quit. A good activist needs time to be inactive. A good community organizer needs space to be away from the community. Making time and space to be alone is essential for coming back and working together.

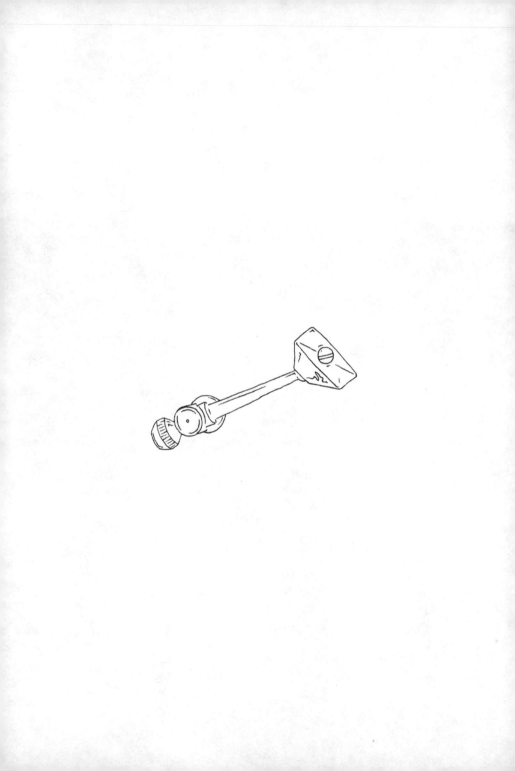

Varying Your Retrieve

I walk down the path behind the dunes that takes me to my favorite jetty. A great blue heron notices me and slowly, clumsily, lifts into the air only to settle back down fifty feet away. The tide is rising, and a slow tongue of water progresses down the path. As my walkway becomes a tidal causeway, I step to the side, careful not to brush my ankles against the green clumps of poison ivy hidden amongst the tan beach grass. It's a bother picking my way through the side brush, but it's also a good sign. When the path is completely covered by water it means that it's dead high tide, and the "schoolies" will start making their trip between the Pamet River and Cape Cod Bay . . . right past my jetty. As I reach the long rocky outcrop, a couple of weekend anglers are already there. I take my place as we cast out into the race, then retrieve our lures back to shore. Cast out and reel in, cast out and reel in, cast out and reel in; the perpetual rhythm of fishing. I do what I usually do and vary my retrieves. First, I cast out and reel in fast, pulling in my weighted rubber sand eel so quickly that it rides the surface. Then I cast out and reel in excruciatingly slow, letting my lure bounce off the bottom. Next, a medium retrieve, keeping the lure in the middle of the water column as best I can. Probably my most productive retrieve incorporates a little twitch or jerk as I raise my rod quickly then return it slowly, giving the line some slack while I reel in. This brings the lure up then lets it drop back down, simulating (at least in my imagination) a wounded baitfish and giving the bigger fish I'm after a chance to hit the bait on its fall. The guy next to me today, however, has just one technique: he casts out his lure as far as he can and cranks it in as fast as possible. Over and over for more than an hour he does exactly the same thing with every cast and retrieve. I catch a good number of schoolies that day. He catches nothing.

Activists can get stuck in tactical ruts. What do we do when we want to express our anger? We march! What do we do when we want to make our case to authority? We distribute a petition! (Or we march!) What do we do when we want media attention? We stage a die-in! (Or, habitually, we march!) There's nothing wrong with marches or petitions or die-ins . . . or strikes, rallies, speeches, pickets, occupations, flash mobs, media pranks, or any other tactics that activists use. The problem becomes when we use them automatically and reactively. I was once running an activist training workshop outside of Austin, Texas when one of the participants, a long-time activist, announced that their group would be holding their 21st Annual March Against the Death Penalty the following weekend. A younger activist beside me innocently remarked, "If you've had twenty marches already, and we still have the death penalty in Texas, don't you think it's time to try something else?" The remark was not well received, but the whippersnapper had a point. Marches are, have been, and can still be visibly powerful displays of people power and an effective way to challenge the powers that be. Think of the Suffrage March in New York City in 1915 (women gained the vote four years later) or the 1963 March for Jobs and Freedom in

Washington, DC, where Martin Luther King gave his famous "I Have a Dream " speech (the Civil Rights Act was passed the next year). But marches don't always work . . . nor do any tactics. What worked this year might not work the next, and what works in one context or with a particular audience might not work with another. The thing is this: you won't know what tactic works best until you try out a whole bunch of different ones.

Study the Shoreline

The first thing I do when I find a new place to fish is study the shoreline. When I began fishing, I'd just show up, cast out anywhere and catch nothing, then watch as other people reeled in fish after fish. Now I've learned to hold back and look. Where are the shady spots? The water lilies? What about that tree that fell at the pond's edge in the big windstorm last week — would that provide good cover for the fish? If I am surf fishing, I look for sand bars and troughs and cuts where the big fish might be hunting baitfish. On the jetty I pay careful attention to the tides and how that impacts the water inflow and outflow between the estuary and bay. And things change. The tides, of course, but also other features. One morning there will be a whole new spread of lily pads just perfect for bass to hide under that wasn't there the day before. Or a storm will have swept away the sandbar that created the trough that was my go-to spot for stripers all summer long. By carefully studying the fish's environment, and working with it instead of casting about blindly, I catch more fish.

The first rule of guerilla warfare is to know your terrain and use it to your advantage. For the Cuban revolutionaries, this meant knowing the mountains of the Sierra Maestra. For the Vietcong, it meant the jungles and deltas of Vietnam. Most activists won't find themselves fighting in mountains or jungles, but the principle is still sound: in order to be effective, you need to study your environment. In the training workshops I help run at the Center for Artistic Activism, we spend an entire afternoon with local activists mapping out their native terrain, filling up poster-size sheets of paper with details of political, social, demographic, geographical, and cultural topography. We map out who holds the power and who or what they are beholden to; the ethnic, tribal, language, and religious groups that populate the area and their relations with one another; the social, religious, labor, and political organizations present and the role they play in society; the age of the population and where they live, work, or go to school. Then there's the cultural landscape: the media people read, watch, or listen to, and the signs, symbols, and stories that resonate with them. Finally, we discuss the shifts taking place in the terrain, asking: What features are ascendant? Which are in decline? Do people still read newspapers? Or has all communication gone online? And how might the answers to these questions differ for different populations? Even for those activists who have worked in the same area, with the same population, on the same issue, for years, this mapping exercise usually reveals features they had overlooked. It's only after studying the terrain that the time is right to think about strategy and tactics, because strategy and tactics only work within context.

Fishing for Life

"Give a person a fish and they eat for the day. Teach a person to fish and they eat for life." That's how the aphorism goes, and after a forty-year hiatus, I had to relearn how to fish. I had a lot of teachers: there were the New England anglers on the Outer Cape beaches who would tell me what popper to be casting out into the surf, the old Chinese men on Manhattan piers who taught me the best technique to get a crab on a hook to catch the tautog lurking under the dock, and then there were my senseis on YouTube: an entire amateur academy online who schooled me in everything from the right technique to work a rubber worm in the lily pads to how to boil up my own catfish bait. But mainly I taught myself how to fish through a lot of observation and reflection, and a lot of trial and error (emphasis on the latter). I discovered that the catfish and carp in Central Park Lake eat only bread balls because that's what the tourists feed the ducks and turtles. I found out that hooking a rubber worm in the middle, "wacky style," may catch more bass, but it also means a lot more swallowed hooks and injured fish. And I also found out that when the fish are biting you can cast out almost anything into the surf and you'll get a hit. Every once in a while, I'll see a novice angler casting out near me. Sometimes, I'll go over to teach them as others have taught me: giving them a few pointers and offering some encouragement.

But I also know that if they are going to fish for life, they are going to have to teach themselves.

A few years back I was eating breakfast in the Washington Square Diner, probably the last remaining diner in my New York City neighborhood, with my friend and fellow founder of the Center for Artistic Activism, Steve Lambert. A student from one of our training workshops walked in, recognized us, and came over to chat. We exchanged the usual pleasantries and then, because we are activists, started talking about activism. He told us he was working on a high-profile campaign to raise the minimum wage for fast food workers. We told him we'd been following the campaign and how impressed we were with the creative tactics they were using. We chatted some more until it was time for him to leave. He was almost out the door when he turned around, came back to our table, and said, "You know, a lot of our tactics and strategy are coming out of what I learned from you all." It was a surprise to us, since none of it closely resembled anything we taught. I think it was even a realization to him. He had so thoroughly made our lessons his own that our contribution was merely an afterthought prompted by seeing us. For the past decade, I've trained people how to be more effective, more affective, and more creative activists. The easiest way for me to do this is teach people how to do what I would do. This shortcut might make a good action, but it won't make a good activist. Teaching a person to be an activist is not about telling them what to do, it's helping them figure out what's best for themselves. This means stepping back from "best practices" and checklists for "what makes a good action" and teaching the underlying principles and philosophies, and demonstrating through case studies and historical examples what good creative activism looks like. I want the activists I train to use what they learn from me, sure, but it's more important that they learn from their own histories and practices, commitments, and talents, and put all this into creating something I could never have created, or even imagined. If this happens they will be activists for life.

It's Not A Competition

When the schoolies are running, my local jetty is lined with anglers. We're respectful of one another and try to give each other room so our lines don't cross, yet it is still obvious when someone has caught a fish, and just as obvious — to me, at least — when I have not. In this situation, it's hard for me not to feel jealous, competitive, and then a bit resentful of these weekenders catching all these fish at my local spot. Who are they to be catching all my fish and leaving me with none? This, of course, is ridiculous. While in the grand scheme, there is a finite number of fish in the sea and the fishing stocks are being depleted, the culprits are climate change and capitalism in the form of huge fishing industry trawlers scooping up fish in international waters, not a few weekend anglers. On the jetty some people catch more and some less, but this is just a matter of having the right lure, a certain amount of skill, and a lot of luck. As people start reeling in fish, and I'm still waiting for a hit, I just remind myself that fishing is not a competition. When the schoolies are running there's enough fish for everyone and all of us end up catching something.

As an activist, it's hard not to get jealous of others' successes. I know I'm not supposed to be competitive with my comrades — Solidarity Forever! — but still, it happens. While my downtown community activist group was struggling to rack up a single win, a group in the Bronx made the papers by saving their community garden; when my nonprofit organization is rejected for its umpteenth grant, we hear of the Ford Foundation making a three-year commitment to supporting a friend's organization. I start to strategize and ask myself: Why are they succeeding and we are not? What might we do so we succeed and they don't? Then, disgusted by the capitalist, competitive thinking that has taken over my brain and constricted my heart, I step back and take a long view. Over the arc of my activist life, I have had successes as well as failures — as have my friend's organization, and likely that gardening group in the Bronx as well. But more importantly, if I step back even further, I can start to see their successes as mine too. Our tactics might differ: I work with creative forms of activism, others use legal or electoral means, and our issues may vary: lately, I've been working on anti-corruption campaigns while admiring my friend's work on the environment, but in the big picture we are all working toward the same goals: a more just and sustainable world. "Diversity of Tactics" has become the norm at most large-scale, multi-group protests these days. At its worst this means marching peacefully with tens of thousands, while a small group of balaclava-wearing, black-clad protestors makes the news by setting fire to an upside-down American flag in front of the Starbucks window they just smashed. But at its best, diversity of tactics is a recognition that there are many approaches to activism and no one way is the best. In fact, it's the diversity of many approaches that is the single best approach.

Sharing the Jetty

I usually get to my favorite fishing jetty early, when I am one of only a few people there. But as the day gets brighter and the tides get closer to their ideal high-water point, the jetty begins to fill up. First is a group of older men, in their seventies at least, speaking quietly amongst themselves in a language I can't place and don't understand. Then come the fishing bros with expensive gear who look at my yard-sale rod and reel with a combination of curiosity and contempt. A mother and her two children show up. She stares at her phone, bored and inattentive, while her daughter and son randomly plop their bait into the water. Finally, a group of a half dozen or more teenagers arrive, talking loudly over music blaring out of the radio they've brought with them, spending equal amounts of time horsing around and casting out. Even with social distancing the jetty gets crowded, and I make way for the newcomers, but not without reservations and a bit of resistance. None of them fish the way I do: they are too loud or too taciturn, too serious or not serious enough. They don't fish with the right lures. (*Everyone* knows that you fish with five-inch Savage Gear Sand Eels in either silver or pearl to catch schoolies on this jetty). But that's not the worst of it. With the wrong lures, the wrong gear, the wrong technique, and the wrong attitudes they sometimes catch more fish than me.

One of the dubious privileges of being white, straight, male, middle class, and from the United States is the belief that your way of doing things is the best way to do things. Nowhere is this more evident than a political meeting where some white dude will stand up and proceed to explain with assurance and authority and volume exactly what the situation is (no matter the situation) and precisely the only possible course of action (invariably, the one they suggest). It's a kind of White Male Universalism, not born of many years of study and experience, testing and evaluation, but simply because your way is the only possible right way of doing things. These days, however, most of the activists I work with are younger, queerer, darker, and poorer than I am. The majority are also female-identified and from outside North America. They have different ways of doing things: different ideas, different approaches, different styles. My first instinct is often to stand up and mansplain how it is and how activism should be done. But I've learned (or rather, I've been taught) to sit down and listen — in activist-speak: "Step up by stepping back." Sometimes other people's ideas turn out to be wrong, but most of the time they are simply different, born of that person's particular experience and position in the world — just as mine are. As more and more activists, the public, and even the power elite look less like me, these "different" ideas may be more in touch with the mainstream than mine are, and this means their approach can be more affective, and therefore more effective, than mine. This doesn't mean that my ideas are simply "male, pale, and stale" and should be summarily dismissed, just that they aren't the only ideas that matter, and may not be the ones that matter most at this moment. After forty-odd years of being an activist, of being someone who teaches activists with assurance and authority, I am no longer the center of activism. Personally, it's uncomfortable. Politically, it's about time.

Using the Wind

Sometimes I have to fish when it's windy, and when the wind is up it is best to cast with it rather than against it. This is pretty obvious. Sometimes, however, you don't have a choice. When surf casting, for instance, if the wind is blowing in from the water, you either cast into it or you go home. Casting into the wind can be done, you just need to use heavier lures and reconcile yourself to the fact that you will not be able to cast out as far. You will also likely spend a fair amount of your fishing time picking wind knots out of your line. But there's another way to deal with the wind. While you can't change the force and direction of the wind, you can change your positioning. If you are fishing in a boat, just cast off the other side. On a stream, move to the other bank, or fish upstream instead of downstream. It may take a bit more time to get downwind when fishing on a pond or lake, but it's usually doable with a walk through the woods. Situated where I am on Cape Cod at its narrowest point, if the wind is blowing the wrong way on the ocean side, I can take a short jaunt to the bay where it's blowing the right way, or vice versa. When I can find a way to work with the wind, fishing is a lot easier: my line snarls less and I can cast much further, and this means catching more fish.

As an activist the wind is often against you. The other side often has more power, money, resources, and an entrenched tradition that we do not, and while it's still possible to win victories, it's always a struggle. It's better to find a way to work with the wind. Favianna Rodriguez, an artist and activist who believes the way to change society is through shifting its culture, once explained to me that why she's such an avid news reader, social media follower, and popular culture fan is because this allows her to gauge which way the prevailing wind is blowing and tailor and time her interventions accordingly. It's in this vein that the radical playwright Bertolt Brecht once wrote that:

> I believe that an artist, even if he sits in strictest seclusion in the traditional garret working for future generations, is unlikely to produce anything without some wind in his sails. And this wind has to be the wind prevailing in his own period, and not some future wind. There is nothing to say that this wind must be used for travel in any particular direction. Once one has a wind one can naturally sail against it; the only impossibility is to sail with no wind at all or with tomorrow's wind.

Brecht's advice was meant for artists, but it works for activists (and anglers) as well. Activism is always easier with the wind in your sails. Understanding which way the wind is blowing and working with it doesn't mean letting it take you wherever it will, it means maneuvering your activism so you can use the wind to your advantage.

Surf Fishing vs. Pond Fishing

Most of my fishing is either surf fishing or pond fishing, and the two could not be less alike. Surf fishing is exciting, exhilarating, and even a bit dangerous. Waves wash over me and the undertow threatens to pull my legs out from under. When the wind is up it howls in my ears and rips the tops off the waves and throws the spray in my face. Each time I get a bite there's always the chance that something massive — a fifty-inch striper or a five-hundred-pound shark — is on the other side of my line (admittedly, neither has ever been the case). Pond fishing is much more tranquil. The water is often calm and glassy, a light breeze rustles the birch leaves that surround the pond, I can hear the insects buzzing and the birds and frogs calling out to one another, and in the early mornings a white mist rises from the surface of the pond. The fishing is different too. Surf side, if the fish are running off the beach, I am likely to catch them. It sometimes takes months until the fish show up, but once they do all I need to do is cast out something shiny and silver and they will bite hard. (In answer to my question, "What's the best lure to catch bluefish?" the guy behind the counter in my local Cape Cod tackle shop, in typical taciturn New Englandese, replied, "A tin can.") Pond fishing takes more finesse, and a different type of patience. The fish are always there, trapped by geography in a limited space, but they just might not be interested in what I have to offer. And even if they are, and they bite, they may just nibble, or take a few passes, or even swallow and spit out my bait before I have time to set my hook. As an inexperienced fisherman, I picked up saltwater fishing pretty easily once I knew when and where the fish were, but I'm still learning how to slowly entice the fish in my local pond, and when to set the hook at the exact right moment so they won't get away. I like fishing in both fresh and saltwater equally, but I've also learned to appreciate how different they are.

There's a difference between activism and organizing. Activism is about attention-grabbing tactics: the protest march, the die-in, or the media prank. If the historical moment is right, these tactics can generate a lot of attention and your issue can move quickly from the margins to the center of public political concern. Organizing, on the other hand, is slow and sly. It entails going to community meetings week after week to get to know local residents and gain their trust, patiently building networks of support and solidarity. While an activist is often front and center, getting their picture in the paper, a good organizer works behind the scenes, barely noticeable. Both are necessary for social change. An activist draws attention to issues that might otherwise be overlooked or ignored. The organizer sets the stage for the activist by creating an environment receptive to their actions and then follows up by turning attention into concrete political gains. Like many newbies, when I was first starting out, I was attracted to activism. It's what I immediately noticed when looking around the political scene, and it's what got people to notice me. As I've aged, my politics have become less ego-driven and I've come to appreciate the often invisible importance of organizing. Without organizing, activism is often just a flash in the pan, light and smoke without lasting effect. Yet without activism, organizing will not ignite public passions. It's not an either/or sort of thing, you need both activism and organizing in order to change the world, but you need to approach each differently.

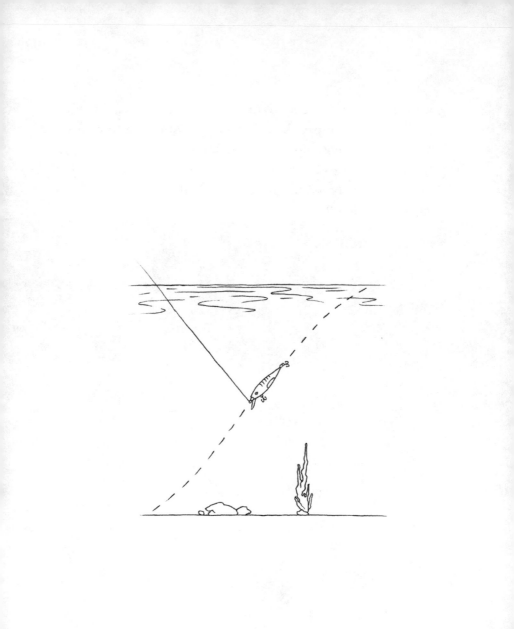

Shallow, Deep, or In Between

It's a spring Saturday and I'm out with my comrades from the Lower East Side Collective in Tompkins Square Park when a young couple, enjoying the day, innocently slows down to look at the pamphlets we have spread across our folding table. Seeing an opportunity, I engage. I begin with an impassioned plea about the necessity of saving community gardens, then move on to a detailed explanation of the varied real estate and governmental interests arrayed against the gardens, segue into a blistering ideological attack on neoliberalism, and conclude with a call for direct action . . . only to be confronted with bewildered looks and the question: "What's a community garden?" My approach made complete sense to *me*, but it didn't acknowledge where *they* were at. Activists often approach people as if they are all at the same level. We make the same pitch, in the same way, to those already on our side as those who have no knowledge of, or interest in, our issues. This one-size-fits-all approach often ends up boring the committed and confusing the uninformed. Working with activists now, I draw from a model developed for public health campaigns. Getting someone to quit smoking, it turns out, entails moving them through a series of steps, from basic awareness of the issue (smoking kills), to them acting on that issue (stop smoking), to having their action on that issue become part of their identity (I am a non-smoker). There are twelve steps in all, and it gets quite complicated, but the principle is quite simple: you need to know where people are in these stages in order to design the most effective approach to reach them. Some people — like the couple I accosted in the park — need their awareness raised, but others don't. They need to know how to act on their awareness, or they need to be confirmed in their identity as someone who already knows and acts. No one approach will reach all the people, all the time; that's why it's critical to use multiple approaches, aimed at multiple audiences, in every campaign.

To catch a fish you have to reach the fish, and this entails, among other things, knowing how deep they are swimming. Anglers call the span from water surface to floor the "water column," and targeting exactly where the fish are is a matter of both science (calculating water temperature and using fish-finding sonar) and common sense (when the surface water heats up the fish tend to go deep, unless, of course, you are fishing for fish who like warm water, who then rise to the top). As Buck Perry, the inventor of the diving spoonplug, is reported to have said, "They're either shallow, deep, or somewhere in between." Once you have a hunch of where the fish are, you need to select the right lure for the depth. If they are up on top, I use a popper or maybe a jerk bait — something that stays on the surface. Down low, I go with weight, often dragging along the bottom of the lake or beach with some sort of sinker. And in the middle, a diving lure is a good bet, or possibly a fast retrieve on a jig. None of this guarantees I'll actually catch a fish, but knowing whether to run deep or shallow makes the odds a bit better.

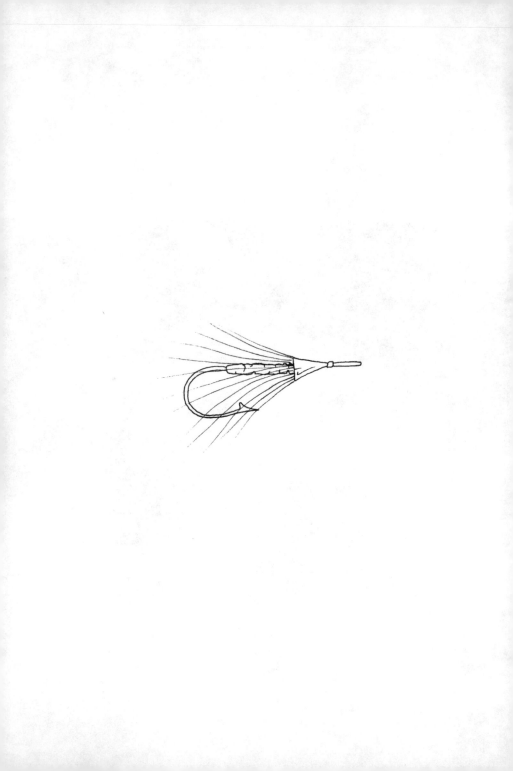

What Fish Like

To figure out what sort of bait a fish is likely to be attracted to I've become a careful observer of their food ecosystem. What flies are hatching? What baitfish are swimming in the shallows? At what stage of growth are the frogs? Are they tadpoles? Pollywogs? Full-grown froglets? Once I've gathered this information, it's a matter of matching my bait to their food. The easiest way to make this match is to use whatever the fish are eating as live bait. But this can be impractical at times (ever try to hook a dragonfly?) and since fishing with live bait usually entails a lot of just waiting while the bait twitches in the water, it is pretty boring too. It's far more fun to fish with artificial lures and they now make ones that are "holographically printed" to look like exact copies of the bait they are replicating. I own a few of these lures myself, and they work pretty well, but I'm pretty convinced that the exacting realism is more for my benefit than it is for the fish's. The truth of the matter is that the lure does not need to look exactly like what it emulates. Fishing flies are made of bird feathers and animal fur, rubber worms can have sparkles, and popper plugs look like cigars. What matters most is that the lure captures the essence of what the fish like, and when it does, they will bite.

As an activist, it is important to understand what people like. Not what you think they should like as fully enlightened beings of the great society yet to come, but what they actually like in the here and now. Looking at popular culture is one way to gain this understanding. In our activist training workshops, after a long day of presentations and exercises, we take participants on a "culture date." Being earnest activists, they usually assume we are going somewhere to watch a documentary on mountaintop removal or to listen to a poetry reading on the malaise of capitalist alienation. This is not what we do. Instead, we take them to whatever it is that non-activists are doing on a weekend night in their locale. We've gone to baseball games, dance clubs, tourist walks, amusement parks, gambling casinos, roadside BBQs, blockbuster action movies, and musical theater. We enjoy ourselves and, more importantly, we watch other people enjoying themselves. Then, the next morning, we discuss why people love this cultural activity and how we might integrate some of what they love into our activism. This is not a simple job of emulation. Just because people love watching *Fast and Furious* movies doesn't mean we should all race muscle cars to our next protest and blow stuff up. We need to look below the surface. *Fast and Furious* is about fast cars and explosions, but it's also about a non-biological, multiracial, rebel "family" who fights the good fight against the corrupt powers that be, which, when you think about it, is not a bad public identity for an activist group to cultivate. By digging deep into the DNA of popular culture we can discover what people like in order to find ways to make activism more likable, and therefore more popular too.

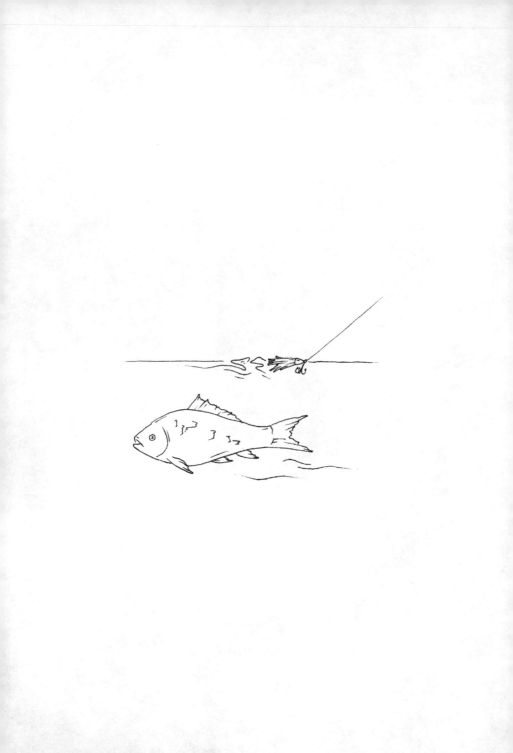

Think Like a Fish

In order to catch fish, you need to learn to think like a fish. When I'm out fishing I think to myself: If I were a fish, what would I want to eat? What time of day would I be hungry? Where would I go to cool down in the heat of the day, or to warm up in the morning? Where might I lurk in search of prey? Where would I feel safe from predators? And then I fish with that bait, at those times, in those spots. A rudimentary knowledge of fish psychology coupled with a careful study of the shoreline results in more bites. But of course I can't think like a fish. I can only think like a human who thinks what a fish might think, and because of this I'll never truly understand fish thinking. I can, however, observe fish behavior and extrapolate from that. So, for instance, when the fish are breaking the surface, I figure this probably means they are hungry. Or where the baitfish are swirling, I conjecture that it's likely the predator fish I'm after are nearby. From these observations, I can build up a simple profile of how a fish might think. Fish aren't necessarily dumb — we just can't understand their thoughts.

In order to convince people of our political point of view and bring them over to our side, we need to know how they think. Some of this can be figured out by observing their behavior: What politicians do they vote for? Do they attend a church, mosque, or temple? What news programs and podcasts do they listen to? But with people we're not limited to just studying behavior and extrapolating thinking. Unlike fish, we can talk to them to find out what they are thinking. This sort of research can be done informally: striking up casual conversations with folks in a bar, nail salon, or fishing spot, or it can be done more systematically through focus groups and surveys. With this knowledge we can tailor our approach using words, symbols, and concerns that resonate with our audiences, and avoid ones that may have negative connotations. Knowing how people think, their motivations and resistances, means we have a much better chance of reaching and convincing them. But there's another benefit to figuring out how people think. Activists sometimes approach people we are trying to reach with a certain contempt. Why don't the masses listen to us? It must be because they are too stupid or too brainwashed to see the obvious truth in front of them. False consciousness! To counter this we yell louder or argue more forcefully, which convinces no one, or we limit our appeals to the "woke" few who already understand and agree. Neither approach helps with social change. Understanding the reasons people have for doing what they do, believing what they believe, and thinking what they think, helps us engage them with the thought and respect they deserve.

React Like a Fish

The problems of trying to think like a fish lie not only with the near impossibility of interspecies empathy, but with the uncertainty surrounding whether fish think much at all. Personally, I have yet to witness a fish pondering. Yes, sometimes they are slow to bite — there's nothing slower than a carp opening its mouth to slowly suck in a bread ball floating on the surface of the water, and yes, fish like to nibble and taste when fishing with live bait, but my hunch is that what looks like slow thinking to me is merely reacting to various stimuli like smell, taste, and movement to them. Often fish don't take time to "think" at all. If fish are feeding and I see a rise and can plop my lure down in the middle of the commotion fast enough, chances are good that I'll be rewarded with an immediate hit. Fish live in a fast, competitive world. They need to eat things that are trying to elude them and, in turn, elude those bigger fish (or anglers) who are trying to eat them. Hesitate a second, and your meal goes by or you turn into a meal yourself. To survive, fish learn to react rather than think: a silver flash means a minnow, a fuzzy something is a nymph, a white underbelly with protruding limbs floating on the surface is a tasty frog. Immediate reactions, not contemplation, means survival. Besides, having killed and cleaned my fair share of fish I can say with certitude that fish brains are just not that big.

A lot of activism is based upon the Enlightenment belief that humans are rational beings who think and then act. Democratic theory is based on this belief, and it's understandable that those of us who would like our society to become more democratic and thoughtful operate under this assumption as well. This is why activists spend so much time on researching reports, composing talking points, and handing out fact-filled flyers. Unfortunately, humans don't think the way we think we think. In fact, most of the time humans are not really consciously thinking at all, we are just reacting to stimuli based upon patterns we've established and beliefs we already hold. This is why no amount of reasonable facts articulated in clever op-eds or laid out on well-designed flyers change people's minds. If those facts don't fit with what we already believe, we tend to ignore them, dismiss them, or twist them to make them fit. "Confirmation bias" is what cognitive scientists call this phenomenon. So what can activists do to counter this? The first thing to do is figure out the patterns that guide people's reaction: the beliefs they have and the stories they tell themselves to make sense of their world. Knowing this, we can then fit the facts we want understood into their beliefs and stories. But we can also disrupt old patterns of thought through actions that defy easy classification and immediate reaction. Take a protest, for instance. When you see a protest, you know immediately what it is and react to it just as immediately. If you like protests and support the cause then you run to join; if you don't then you immediately move away. In either case, there's not much thinking going on. This is why it's good to create protests that don't look like protests. This is what Reclaim the Streets activists in London, England did in the early 1990s when they created anti-car protests that looked and felt like a dance parties, and it's what environmentalists in Chongqing, China did in 2014 when they staged a public marriage ceremony while wearing gas masks to protest government inactivity on smog control. When the protest pattern is broken, reaction time slows down, and thinking has a chance. People can learn to think before reacting. We have big brains.

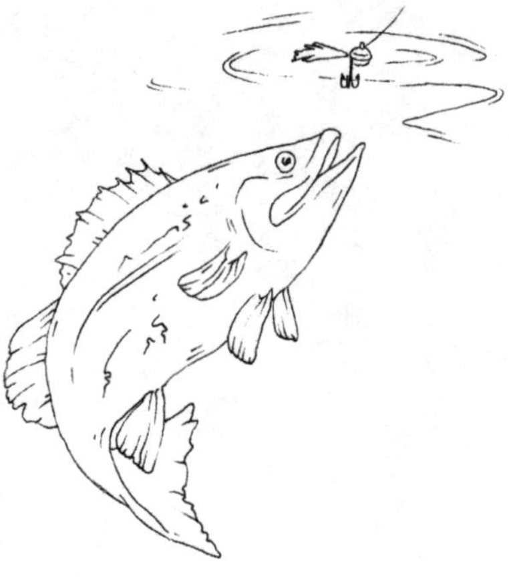

Act Like a Fish

While waiting for a bite, I spend a lot of time trying to think what a fish might think is a tasty treat. I also try to figure out what a fish might react to in order to provide exactly the right stimuli. I sometimes even go as far as trying to imagine what a fish might be feeling to get a feel for what might satisfy their hunger. But, again, all this is speculation. I can never really know what a fish thinks or feels or what will trigger a reaction. There is, however, one thing I can know for certain: whether a fish bites or not. When it comes down to it, this is really all that matters. A fish may be thinking that my lure looks like a fish or grub they are hunting, and feel that it would be good to eat, or may not be thinking or feeling at all, but none of this really matters to me unless they commit to the action of chomping on my bait. It's that simple: if the fish bites then I have a good chance of catching it, if it doesn't, I have no chance. No one wants to hear a fish story that details the psychology of a fish but ends with an empty reel.

Activists give a lot of thought to changing people's hearts and minds about issues. We try to "raise awareness" through pamphlets, soapbox speeches, press releases, social media posts, and other educational tactics, and we try to rouse people's emotions through street protests, vigils, media stunts, creative interventions, and other affective tactics. Underlying this emphasis on hearts and minds is a faith that thoughts and feelings will somehow automatically lead to action. This, I've come to believe, is a misplaced faith. In our consumer-spectator society, we are used to ingesting all sorts of radical ideas and ideals without ever acting upon them. In myriad ways, from critical lessons taught in school to progressive dramas we watch on Netflix, we are taught to think the correct thoughts and feel the right feelings, then we exit the classroom or get up from the couch, leave these lessons behind, and get on with our lives doing pretty much what we were doing before. This is not to say that changing thinking and feeling are not important for social change. It is "a necessary but not sufficient condition," in social science speak, and people need to think that something is wrong and feel they can change it before change can happen. The goal, however, is always the change, and without people acting things stay the same. This is why it's so important for activists to do more than merely raise awareness and stir up passions. We need to pay equal attention to creating opportunities and charting pathways for people to act on their thoughts and feelings. Activists are in the business of getting people to act.

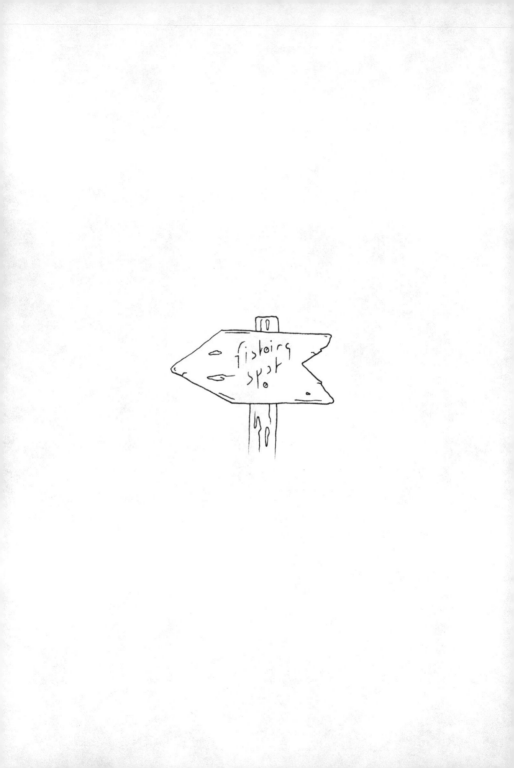

Ask the Locals

As much as I like to think of myself as a modern, enlightened male I am still loath to ask for directions from strangers. I've learned, however, that to catch fish you need to ask for advice all the time. If I'm new to an area, the first thing I do is go to the local tackle store and ask whoever is there a whole bunch of questions: What's biting? Where are they biting? What are they biting on? They always have good answers, though the style of delivery can vary quite a bit depending on the locale. In the only remaining tackle shop in Manhattan, there's a fast-talking, loquacious kid who engages me for twenty minutes about the merits of homemade bread balls vs. store-bought boilies to catch carp in Central Park Lake (bread balls win). Out on the Cape, the advice is delivered in monosyllabic pulses that go something like this: Are the fish biting? Yup. Where? Off the ocean side beaches. Which beach? Ballston. What are they biting on? Depends. Depends on what? And so on, but with perseverance and a bit of patience I always find out what I need to know to catch fish. Other anglers can be good sources of intel too, but anglers are also notorious liars: exaggerating their own fishing prowess and jealously guarding their favorite fishing spot (*mea culpa*). Likewise, tackle shop employees are in the business of selling gear, so I always consider what is being said and who is saying it and take advice with a grain of salt. But to catch fish, local knowledge is invaluable.

Democratic social change demands popular participation, and it's an activist's job to educate, inspire, and motivate people. To do this you need to understand them, not as an abstraction — *The People!* — but as real people, living in real places with real lives. This takes local knowledge. The importance of this was brought home to me on Gorée, a small island off the coast of Dakar, Senegal. It's a beautiful place with sandy beaches and bright, whitewashed buildings and an ugly past as a disembarkment point for African slaves bound for the Americas. Today, Gorée is mainly a tourist attraction. I was there as part of a workshop organized in partnership with West African trainers, and we were working with a group of artists, activists, and investigative journalists involved in a campaign to combat corruption. We were planning on doing a training action at the end of the week-long session, yet none of us were from the island. Cheikh "Keyti" Sene, one of the trainers (and co-creator of the popular Sengalese rap news show *Journal Rappé*) quickly identified the problem and came up with an exercise to address it. He instructed the workshop participants to wander the island that afternoon and do research. The French and Wolof speakers were to interview locals and talk to them about how corruption impacts their personal lives, while we English speakers observed where people hung out and what they did. In the evening, we reconvened and shared what we learned. From talking to locals we identified a target: corrupt officials who were receiving kickbacks for allowing locals to act as guides to visiting tourists. Through our observations, we found a good location for our intervention: a prominent sculpture across from the ferry landing where tourists come ashore. Our eventual action, like most practice actions, was of limited impact in effecting change on the island, but what did change, for the activists as well as me, was our awareness of the importance of local knowledge.

Night Fishing

F ish are often active at night; it's their prime hunting and feeding time. The best surf fishing, for instance, usually starts at dusk and stretches into the night and gets even better the darker it gets, especially if there's only a new moon or no moon at all. Fishing in the pitch black, however, is challenging. I never realized how much I rely upon my vision for fishing until I started going out at night. When I cast I like to see where my lure lands: Did it fall short of the mark or did it go wide? When I retrieve I like to see the action of the lure in the water: Is it bobbing or diving or weaving in the way I want? And when I snarl my line, I like to be able to see the knot so that I can pick it apart with my fingernails and get back to fishing. All of this sensory feedback is absent at night. Other senses do fill in. You rely much more upon feel and even hearing when you can't see a fish hit your plug, but there's been a few times when I mistook the curiosity of a passing seal for the hit of a monster striped bass (luckily seals are smarter than fish and usually don't get hooked). In time, my other senses will likely get sharper, and with practice I'll know better how far I've cast and be able to distinguish stripers from seals, but for now, for me, fishing in the dark means fishing blind.

Activism can sometimes seem like fishing in the dark. You go out and do your action and hope for the best. Your message might reach the right people, get some media coverage, have an impact — you might hook a big one — but it'll be more luck than anything else. Some of this uncertainty is endemic to the nature of activism, where so many of the variables that add up to social change are outside of your control, but you can increase your luck by increasing the amount of sensory feedback you receive. When we stage public practice actions in our workshops, we always assign people to be observers and interviewers. As our action happens, the observers stand back and watch the crowd. Who stops and who doesn't? Do they smile, frown, talk to their friends or take pictures? At what points during the action do they do this? And when do they walk away? Meanwhile, interviewers approach passersby to ask questions: Why did they stop to watch? Or why didn't they stop? Do they understand what is going on? What do they think or feel about what is going on? Do they plan on doing anything as a result? Halfway through the practice action we stop. At this point, people usually want a break anyway, and as we have a snack and a drink, we hear the feedback from the observers and the interviewers. Based on this information we tweak the second half of the action. Then, after it's all done, we have a debrief where we discuss what we learned that we might apply to future actions, and how we might use these insights to become better activists. This sort of feedback is essential, otherwise activists are forever acting in the dark.

Après Fish

O ne of the most important parts of activism is what happens after the action. The planning is over, the action has occurred, and now's the time to make sense of it all. Many of my action debriefs have happened in dark bars as we let go of our pent-up anxieties into glasses of beer, but the one I recall most vividly (perhaps because of the lack of alcohol) took place in the brilliant sunshine in the courtyard of a community center in the Jamestown neighborhood of Accra, Ghana. We had just finished an action drawing attention to governmental corruption, and the group of young artistic activists from across West Africa gathered themselves in a big circle. First, we recounted some of the highlights: the kids who spontaneously got involved, the grumpy market woman who ended up staying to watch, the necessity of adlibbing when we realized that a very arty component of the performance just wasn't going to work. But soon the group settled down to the analytic business of the debrief. Everyone went around and gave a short statement of what they observed. Then they went around and talked about what they felt. After these insights, the young activists began their analysis: What worked? What didn't? What surprised us? Finally, they were ready to address the all-important question: What could we do better next time? It's fun to get together after the action and relive the glory moments of what just happened, but the debrief is really about looking forward to the next time.

One of my favorite fishing experiences took place after the fishing was done. My younger son, Sebastien, had invited his friend, Tejas, to stay with us for a long weekend on Cape Cod and they wanted to go surf fishing. I roused the drowsy teens at five o'clock. The romantic mist that surrounded the house as we left at dawn turned into a blowing drizzle when we got to the beach. The surf was up, with large breakers slamming down on the shore and drenching from below any part of our bodies that was not getting wet from above. My son's friend had never fished before, but Sebastien taught him the basics of surf casting and in no time Tejas was casting his lure out past where the waves were breaking and into the relative calm where the striped bass were lurking. Or should have been lurking. Or perhaps were lurking but definitely not biting. We stayed on the beach, casting out and reeling in, without a single bite, getting wet and cold for about an hour and then, by mutual consent, packed it in. On the way home, we stopped for breakfast at a local diner and each of us ordered "The Breaker," a local take on the classic egg, cheese, and bacon sandwich made with linguica sausage, scrambled eggs, and American cheese on a grilled Portuguese sweet roll. (The Portuguese have been the backbone of the local fishing industry since they settled on the tip of the Cape in the mid-1800s.) We sat at the diner for an hour drying out, drinking coffee and tea and eating our heart-attack-on-a-bun, recounting our recent fishing experience, our bad luck, and the fish strike that turned out to be a clump of seaweed. We talked about summer plans and worries about the new high schools they would be attending in the fall. We laughed a lot. By the end of our breakfast, despite the cold and the wet and the absolute lack of fish we caught, Tejas was talking about the next time he might go fishing.

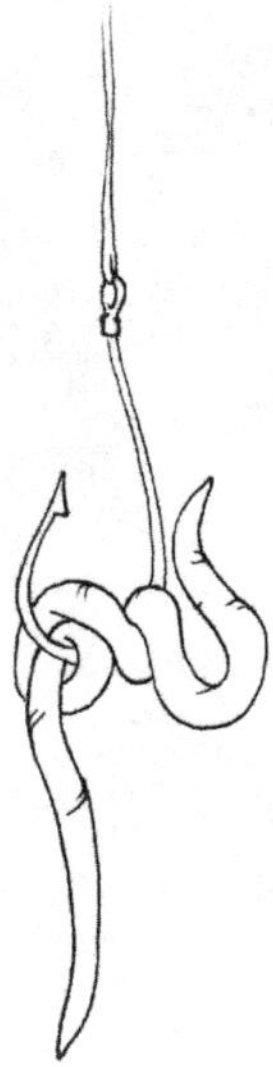

Worms Work

I don't like fishing with live worms. To begin with, the worms themselves are disgusting. They are the color of chicken liver and about the consistency as well, but unlike chicken liver they are always squirming and coiling, and moving frontward and backward, though it's hard to tell which is which. Then I hook them and they squirm some more, exuding dirt-crap out of what I now discover is their backsides. Wriggling on my hook, I cast the worm out into the water and wait, doing nothing except staring at my bobber until a fish, attracted by the theater of cruelty I've staged below the surface, decides to bite. Or nibble, slowly and steadily stripping the worm off the hook so I have to go through the whole disgusting process of re-worming again. I would swear off fishing with worms except for one thing: worms work. Really, really well. When nothing else is catching fish, threading a writhing worm onto a hook and tossing it out into the water is almost guaranteed to get you a fish. It's wonderful to have a perfect cast, a skillful retrieve, and an artful lure, but in the end, the goal is catching a fish.

The "artistic activism" I specialize in gets a lot of attention these days. For good reason, too. It goes back to that first rule of guerrilla warfare I mentioned before: know your terrain and use it to your advantage. Today's political landscape is made up of signs and symbols, stories and spectacles, and activists have begun to realize that working successfully on this terrain necessitates becoming more creative in tactics and strategies. Artistic activism is also new and flashy and fun, and this helps its popularity too. Yet, at times I have my doubts. I've been doing and teaching this sort of activism for more than two-and-a-half decades, and I will likely continue for another two-and-a-half, but a little voice in my head keeps asking the question: Does it work? That's a hard question to answer for all sorts of reasons, but an important question to ask, for what really matters is achieving objectives and winning campaigns, and if artistic activism is not working then there are other things that might. Phone banking, canvassing door-to-door, lobbying politicians and meeting with their aides, attending and speaking up at community meetings are old, dull, and tedious tactics, but they sometimes work better than what's flashy, fun, and new. A good activist needs to be open to a whole range of tactics, both fashionable and old-fashioned, and always ask themselves: Do I just want to do what's new, flashy and fun, or do I want to win?

Old Gear, New Line

I like to boast I own some of the best fishing gear ever manufactured . . . circa the year I was born. Like many anglers, I love trolling yard sales and browsing eBay for deals on rods and reels, and this means that most of my gear is, to use a genteel word, "vintage." For freshwater, my go-to spinning reel is the Model T of fishing reels, the French-made Mitchell 300: indestructible, millions sold, and available in any color as long as it's black. My rod is a medium-light seven-feet Fenwick Feralite in standard Fenwick mud brown. When I'm bayside, I fish with a Penn 710Z, the one with the flashy faux-gold hardware, and an eight-feet Garcia Conolon that had its tip broken off and repaired. For surfcasting I have an eleven-feet custom rod (custom built for someone else) on which I've mounted an old "greenie" Penn Spinfisher 704. I also possess equally venerable offshore, ultralight, baitcasting, and fly-fishing tackle. Using old gear has its downsides: bail springs frequently break and rod windings unwind, but I know that any gear that's already survived fifty-five odd years will usually last the abuse I'll give it over a fishing season. There's one thing, however, I use new and change regularly: my line. I'm not one of those fetishists who replaces their line every few weeks as soon as it gets curly, but I've had enough fish break my line to know that having brand new line casts more easily, snarls less readily, breaks less frequently, and lands more fish.

There are tried and true tactics in activism: the mass protest, the strike, the sit-in, the boycott, the petition, the door-to-door canvas, etc. These old tactics still work, and every activist should be practiced in using them, yet it's important to remember that at one time these old tactics were once new innovations. The petition was perfected in the Chartist struggles for universal suffrage in England in the mid-nineteenth century, and the sit-in was pioneered as a sit-down by auto workers in Detroit in the 1930s and then honed by the US Civil Rights movement in the 1960s. They were tactics created to respond to specific circumstances. The paper petition was, in part, a reaction to the violent suppression of in-person mass protests and uprisings, and the sit-in was in response to union strikers and Black diners being locked out of the businesses they were protesting. In short, new tactics were created because new situations called for them. What made sense then holds true today: activists need to create new tactics to fit new times. But innovation doesn't always mean creating entirely new tactics — sometimes it means putting a new spin on old ones. In our age of entertainment, how might a picket line be reimagined as a performance? With more of our public spaces online, how can a sit-in be carried out virtually? At a time of social distancing, how could a street protest be staged safely? Old tactics are fine, we just need to make sure our thinking is new.

Better with Beer and Friends

Fishing is largely a solitary activity. That's why I gravitated towards it as an introverted pre-teen and then again during a time of social distancing during a pandemic. Yet some of the best times I've had fishing are with other people: dropping lines on a party-boat with my family, listening to my older son sharing his ambivalence about becoming an adult as we stand at water's edge at my favorite pond, or most recently, an evening excursion with my old activist friend Andrew Boyd, talking and casting, casting and talking, as we walked along the jetty where I usually fish alone. I never seem to catch much when I fish with other people, but that's not really the point — the point is spending time with one another. Andrew and I gossiped about other activists we knew and analyzed past campaigns we had worked on together. We discussed the strange state of politics at the present and made our projections for the future. We laughed at our bad luck fishing. And we stood silently together, drinking beer, as the sun set and the sky turned red over the tip of the Cape.

Activism is inherently collective, but not always social. We work together, but sometimes forget to enjoy one another's company. Many times, I've seen this separation between activist life and social life result in burnout as activists, increasingly consumed by their activism, feel as if they "have no life." Neglecting social life causes problems for activist recruitment too, since others, who would like to have a social life, take one look at activists and want nothing to do with the lifestyle they see. By losing people and not gaining others, movements and campaigns wither and die. It doesn't have to be this way: sociality can be built into activism. We did this with the Lower East Side Collective, a community activist group I helped start in New York City in the mid-1990s. LESC was composed of multiple "working groups." One worked on gentrification and rent control, another on protecting community gardens, a third on policing and public life, and so on. Then there was The Ministry of Love. The sole purpose of this group was to make sure we had fun. The Ministry demanded we hold our meetings in back rooms of bars and cafes and then, when the meeting was done, moved everyone to the front to hang out and socialize. It organized trips to baseball games at Yankee Stadium and threw dance parties at a local community center. Most importantly, The Ministry of Love made sure no one ever came to a meeting without being greeted or left without feeling, well, loved. As we grew as an organization, gained more members, racked up more victories and sustained more losses, we came to realize this play group was what made the other groups work.

Snarls

Sometimes when casting, particularly when the wind is up and you are using a light lure, your line snarls. This usually happens at the worst moment. My top three memorable line snarls: 1) standing on the beach with a massive knot in my line and looking out to the surf as a school of stripers swim by; 2) dropping a critical part of my reel overboard while attempting a field "fix" of a snarled spindle; 3) watching people to the left and right of me reel in fish after fish as I stare down at a bird's nest of braided line (this has happened so many times it has congealed into one nightmarish memory). When you get a snarl, you need to take the time to pull the knots apart, picking at the strands with your fingernails and tracing back the loops to locate the ur-knot at the root of it all, before you can resume fishing. Sometimes, however, this is impossible because it's too dark to see, or the knot is too tight, or the fish are biting — right now! — and you simply can't wait. When this happens you need to cut the snarl out, retie your lure, and start again.

There are always snarls in activism: conflicts internal to the organization, often having to do with decision-making and group dynamics, that bring everything to a halt until they get sorted out. These snarls can be caused by leadership struggles as the authority of one faction is contested by another, or by conversations over ideology, strategy, and the "correct line" to take in opinion and actions, and in everyday interactions as some people (often white men) explain too much and others don't feel heard. Most of the time it's worth working these things out. Groups will not grow unless all people are heard and respected and others step back and let others talk and lead. Organizations will not be effective unless systems of power are clarified and agreed upon by all. And while I'm dubious about a "correct line," it is important to untangle differing ideas about strategy, tactics, and ideology. But sometimes picking apart these snarls takes over the entire efforts of a group. This tendency is exacerbated by the desire in many progressive groups to "reach consensus" through "participatory democracy" where everybody speaks and no one listens to one another. (In the sardonic words of social movement scholar Francesca Polletta: "Freedom is an Endless Meeting.") When this happens, activity turns inward and the activist aims of changing the world outside get lost. Sometimes you need to fix organizational snarls, but sometimes you need to cut them out and move on.

Beginnings and Endings

My best days fishing are often those when the beginnings and endings are not in my control. They begin when the sun rises or the sun sets, and I fish until the fish stop biting and go to the deeper, cooler levels of the lake or it gets too dark to see where I am casting. These permeable boundaries are radically different from the rest of my hyper-scheduled, time-managed life. When I'm not fishing, I'm up at 5:00 a.m. to make coffee for myself and respond to emails. Then, at 6:00: I make tea for my wife; 6:15: walk the dog around the block; 6:30: wake the kids up for school and make them smoothies for breakfast; 7:30: be in my office at my desk (having stopped at 7:25 at the cart outside my university building for a cup of coffee — milk, no sugar — already waiting, prepared for me by one of the young Egyptian men who work the stand and know my schedule); 8:00: prep for lectures; 9:30: teach my first class, and so on, throughout the day, with time carefully allotted in minute and hour blocks until I go to sleep at 10:00 p.m., or earlier if I've dozed off in front of the TV watching one of the Scandinavian noir mysteries I'm addicted to. But when I am out fishing — on those days when I have allowed myself more than an "allocated fishing time" — segmented time dissolves deliciously into flowing time, where beginning and endings are expansively elastic.

After suffering through too many endless meetings and dispiriting protests, I've come to realize that one of the worst things an activist can do is be too elastic about time. When meetings don't end on time people get antsy, begin looking at their watches and ignoring the business at hand, and then start slipping out the back to get on with their lives. Soon the only people left in the meeting to make decisions are people who have no other lives to get to — hardly the people you want leading the revolution. Protests, too, need clear beginnings and endings. In order for everyday people to take part in protests, they need to fit them into their everyday schedules, otherwise it will only be those without schedules, the bohemians and trust funders, who can take part. Again, hardly the people you want running the revolution. Action endings are also critical. I can't tell you how many protests I've witnessed — and, regrettably, how many I've helped plan — whose ending was scripted not by activists, but instead by the police breaking up the march or hauling away the protestors. Sometimes there's nothing to be done about this and sometimes, as with planned civil disobedience, this police "ending" is part of our narrative, but usually, it's the result of inattentive timing as we just go on as long as the authorities will let us, which means letting them write the conclusion of our protest story. And, in this ending, they always win.

Too Much Mung

There are times when there is just too much mung in the water to fish. Mung, or Pylaiella as it is officially known, is a foul-smelling brownish, reddish seaweed that rolls up in huge blooms off beaches on the Outer Cape and up and down the New England coast. Mung wraps itself around anything and everything. I throw out a topwater lure and a minute later I am hauling back a football-sized ball of soft brownish goo. I try bottom fishing with bait, and my bait, sinker, and entire line get coated with the stuff. I've had my rod bend double, thinking that I've got a hit, only to realize that the "fish" I caught was the accumulation of ten pounds of mung. What to do? I can keep fishing, knowing that I'll catch nothing and likely get more and more frustrated. I can go home and give up for the day. Or I can prop up my rod in a sand spike, crack a beer, sit on the beach, enjoy the sound of waves crashing and the feeling of the setting sun and ocean breeze on my skin, and scan the shore for good fishing spots to try next time. I've done all three. The only good thing about mung is that it disappears as suddenly as it appears and depending on wind direction and water conditions it may be gone by the next day's fishing.

There are times when conditions are just not right for activism. I remember one time and place in particular. It was in the early 2000s during the upsurge of alternative globalization protests taking place around the world. The World Economic Forum, a cabal of global elites who meet annually to decide the fate of the world, had forsaken their usual meeting place of Davos, Switzerland for New York City and we were there to protest. Our group's contribution to the mass protest was, we thought, a particularly clever and creative action involving tango dancing and martini sipping while marching and dancing under a banner that read: "Bad Capitalist. No Martini. WEF Go Home." When the day of the protest came and we got out onto the street we quickly realized that the police had out-strategized us. They immediately and aggressively arrested anyone they identified as a leader, and hemmed in and divided the rest of the thousands of protesters — including us — into a series of quarter-block long pens separated by broad no man's lands. It didn't matter how clever and creative our action was, we were not going to be able to pull it off that day. Sometimes the weather is against us. A cold, driving rain in Washington, DC during a protest at the inauguration of George W. Bush made us miserable and limited spectators to our miserable selves. And sometimes the timing is not right. In the aftermath of 9/11, when the smell of the smoldering towers pervaded the city and every street corner was crowded with pictures of loved ones who were still missing, it just didn't seem right to be protesting the buildup to the absurd war in Iraq in our usual absurdist ways. Faced with adverse conditions we sometimes went ahead, finding new — more creative or somber — ways to protest; sometimes we went home (or to jail) and sometimes we reconvened in a bar to complain about the bad conditions and plan for our next action when those conditions changed.

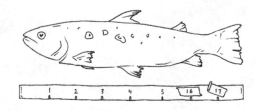

Fish Stories

Fish stories are an integral part of fishing. Anglers love to tell one another about the fish we caught and the ones that got away, usually exaggerating the size and the weight and the duration of the fight in the telling. It's a way of bonding . . . and bragging. It's also sometimes pretty annoying, especially when you've been fishing for hours and aren't catching anything and someone comes up and tells you that you should have been there last night, or earlier that morning, or last Thursday when the fish were biting like mad and they caught an improbable eighteen-inch rainbow trout. But what's more interesting than the stories anglers tell each other are the ones we don't: tales of the hours put in at water's edge catching nothing. The time spent scanning the water for rises that might, just might, mean that a hungry fish is down there under the surface. The repetitive, monotonous, meditative state of casting and retrieving over and over again. Fish stories are all about the glorious event — catching the fish — and they are rarely about the necessary process: fishing.

The tip of Cape Cod is famous as a respite for radicals. It's said that the journalist Jack Reed owned the house down the road from mine and then sold it to Margaret Sanger, the reproductive rights activist, when he left for Russia to join the revolution. Noam Chomsky used to spend his summers in the next town over, and at the dinner parties of older friends I attend, much of the conversation involves reminiscing about the Madison, Wisconsin chapter of the Students for a Democratic Society in the late 1960s. Whenever I give a talk at the local library about contemporary activism, our family makes a wager on how many minutes will pass in the Q&A session before someone prefaces their question with, "In the '60s, we . . ." (fifteen minutes was the longest). While these stories can be annoying, storytelling is part of activism. Activists are forever telling other activists what it was like at the Selma March in '65, or the student uprisings in '68, or battling the World Trade Organization (WTO) in Seattle in '99, or Occupy Wall Street in 2011, or the beginnings of Black Lives Matter in Ferguson in 2014, or . . . Invariably it was more exciting, more effective, and all-around better than it is now. What gets lost in these stories of spectacular actions is all the hard, boring, unexciting work that went into making the event. What's also overlooked is how each of these movements built on what came before. Black Lives Matter is built upon the Black Power movement, which came out of the Civil Rights Movement, which arose from . . . and so on back through history. There are peaks in activism: the marches and protest that make it into the history books and are retold while slurping local oysters at dinner parties on decks on the Outer Cape, but you need to be active all the time, even when it seems as if nothing is happening, if these notable actions are to happen in the first place.

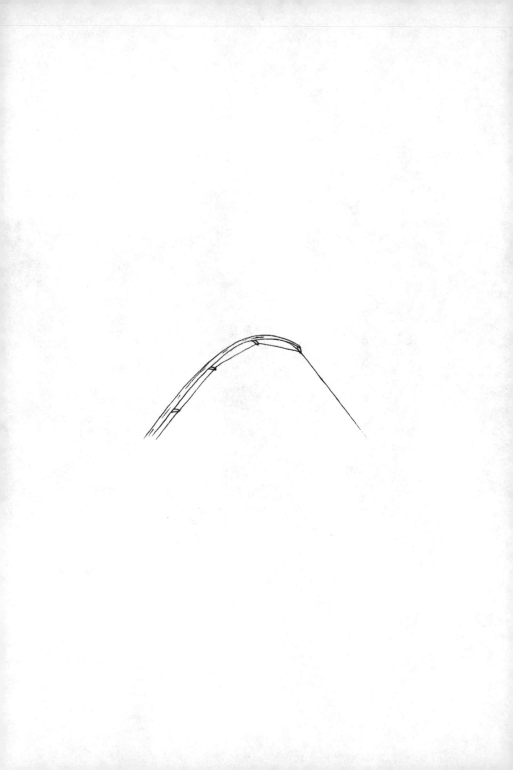

The Thrill

Why is catching a fish so thrilling? I think about this a lot — usually in those non-thrilling moments when I am not catching any fish. I've come to the conclusion that fishing is like gambling: you never quite know when you are going to get a bite. I fish and fish and fish and nothing, and then wham: I get a bite and my adrenaline starts pumping. It's hitting the jackpot. But fishing isn't like slot machine gambling, where some mechanical ratchet or digital algorithm determines your payout (though the terrible odds are similar); it's more like poker, where skill and practice increase your luck. Yes, fishing can be thrilling at times, but at other times, most of the time, it can be excruciatingly tedious. The same repetitive motions, staring across the water, not knowing if there's anything under that opaque surface that might be remotely interested in what I am offering. It is these long stretches of tedium — the runs of bad luck — that make the moment when a fish hits my lure and my reel drag screams as the hooked fish makes its run so incredibly thrilling.

It is hard to describe the rush of being in the middle of a mass demonstration, the feeling you get when you are in the middle of what would normally be a car-jammed boulevard and everywhere you look you see people protesting for the same cause. It's those moments when you viscerally feel the power of the people and experience the thrill of activism. For a bunch of folks, that's all activism is. Some activists get addicted to the thrill and spend their time hopping from one hotspot to another, this protest to that protest, in search of a high. Then there are the thrill addicts who continually raise the stakes in search of new thrills, staging more and more confrontational tactics in order to provoke more extreme responses from authorities and boost their media notoriety. Most common, however, are those activists who quit activism when the thrill is gone. What all these folks don't seem to realize, or don't want to recognize, is that it's the long stretches of patient planning and organizing — the boring meetings, the tedious communications, the uncomfortable fundraising — that allow for the thrilling moments of activism to happen and make them all the more thrilling when they do.

Fish Here Now

When the fish are biting, I stop noticing everything else around me. My eyes are focused on my line and my hands are sensitive to the smallest pull on the rod — I'm in the moment completely. When the fish are not biting, when they are ignoring my fancy lures and couldn't care less about my elegant casts, the world comes back in. When I first began fishing, all I wanted to do was to get back to that peak state of fish catching, but lately I have been enjoying being just as present in the stillness and scenery surrounding me. Watching the sunrise over an oceanside beach or set over the bay, or taking in the sight of the mist rising off the lake in ghostly wisps. Noticing the osprey as she flaps her giant wings and glides in big loops overhead or the resident snapping turtle making his early morning rounds of the circumference of the pond, uncomfortably near my bare legs. Or letting myself be amazed by hundreds of pogies (a type of herring) swirling in an underwater mosh pit just yards offshore the beach. Being in the moment, whatever that moment has to offer, has extended the pleasure I get in fishing from a few highs to the entire experience.

Like catching fish, victories in activism are few and far between. This is why it is important to not only learn to live with the process of activism — the meetings, the strategy sessions, the actions, the postmortems — but to learn to love it. This can be hard sometimes, as anyone who has sat through a multi-hour planning meeting can attest. It's easy to focus on the droning self-important pontification and the excruciating procedures of democracy and wish it was all over and done with so we could just move on and get out on the street. But being stuck in a meeting wishing and hoping you could be somewhere else means missing what is happening there at the moment. There is real beauty in a group of people coming together and sharing their ideas in order to change the world and it's important to notice and appreciate this as well. Being present, however, does not mean being passive and merely accepting things just as they are. Activists are in the business of change and we can — and should — change norms of activist culture to amplify the beauty of creative companionship and minimize the drag of endless meetings. Still, it's *all* a part of activism and, in the words of the LSD-laced college professor turned yogi philosopher Ram Dass, it is important to Be Here Now.

Fish Where Fish Are

First rule of fishing: fish where the fish are and not where they aren't. It sounds obvious, but it's something I had to learn. When I took up fishing again the running joke in my family was that I was the world's worst fisherman. I enjoyed the time by myself, I appreciated the nature around me, but I caught nothing, day after day. Then one day, as I was fishing a local jetty on the bay side of the Outer Cape, I caught a small striped bass, no more than twelve inches long. It was my first fish of the season. Hell, it was my first fish since I had taken up fishing again. I tossed it back, and twenty minutes later I caught another, this one about eighteen inches. Then another, and another, and another. Some small, some big (though none hitting the legal twenty-eight to thirty-five inch "slot" dictated by the Massachusetts Department of Fish and Game that would allow me to keep and eat it). Overnight, I went from the world's worst fisherman to, well, a man actually catching fish. What changed? Not the gear I was using: it was the same old eight-foot Garcia Conolon rod and Penn 710Z reel. Nor was it the lure: I was casting out the same five-inch, white and silver, rubber Savage Gear Sand Eel the guy at tackle store recommended. And it wasn't my retrieve: I was practicing the same jerk, let it drop, reel-in retrieve I had always been using. What changed was the fish. Or, more precisely, the location of the fish: I was where they were.

An activist needs to go where people are. One of my first jobs as an activist was working for an organization that helped organize large protest marches and rallies in Washington, DC. These usually took place on weekends when it was easy for other activists to get there. We'd arrive in a string of rented buses, assemble ourselves, and then march for hours amongst the government buildings, arriving back at the place we began to hold a rally. People Power on public display! Except for one thing: there was no public. The Capitol on weekends is largely a ghost town, so we marched, chanted, rallied, and protested primarily for the benefit of ourselves and a few news crews (that became fewer over time, as the "March on Washington" became a predictable ritual). Where were the people we were trying to persuade and pressure? Doing the things that people usually do on weekends. They were at shopping malls or sporting events, laundromats and farmers' markets, bars or movie theaters, taking walks through leafy parks, maybe even fishing. It's at these public places, where the public actually is, that activists need to be active. Of course, the tactics used need to match the setting. A mass protest is probably not appropriate in a tranquil park, but a natural setting could be a great place to set up an interactive exhibit on the effects of climate change. But like the proverbial tree in the woods, neither a big march nor an intimate exhibit is going to have an impact if no one is around to experience it.

Fish Move On

It was early June when the schoolies arrived, and for a few glorious weeks I was in fishing heaven, catching fish after fish, day in and day out, believing that it was only a matter of time before I caught a "slot fish" big enough to keep and eat (I never did). The jetty filled up with people who were also catching fish, and I was catching so many that I started wearing a rubber glove on my left hand in order to grab the slippery, spiny stripers, unhook them, and get them back into the bay as quick as I could before casting out again. Then one day, fishing at the same place, at the same tide, with the same gear, lure, and retrieve I caught just a few fish, then the next day only a couple, then one, and then none. Every few days for the rest of the summer I would head down to the bay and go out on my jetty to fish. It was still a beautiful place to cast out and unwind, even more so since I was now often the only person fishing, and every once in a great while I'd catch some errant striper who had lost its way, but the fish had moved on for the season.

Being an activist means accepting there will be times of great activity and times when it seems like nothing is happening at all. Having been an activist for most of my adult life I've lived through several of these cycles. I became an activist during an upsurge of organizing on college campuses aimed at divesting from firms that did business with the apartheid regime of South

Africa. My activism soon spilled into other areas. As my fellow students and I looked closer to home, we began protesting the budget cuts that were just beginning to devastate the public university system. At the State University of New York where I did my undergraduate studies, we occupied buildings in the state capital, then at the City University where I was a graduate student, we took to the streets. It was exciting and exhilarating, I felt like I was on the cusp of something. And then nothing: student activists graduated and the protests fizzled. Next, there was the upsurge in angry, joyful, creative activism that surrounded ACT UP as activists, many new to activism, flooded the streets, occupied pharmaceutical buildings, and staged brilliant media zaps to bring attention to the AIDS crisis, the government's inactivity, and the profiteering health care system. Every day it seemed like I was in a mass meeting or at a raucous demonstration. And then the day came when the meetings got smaller and the demonstrations largely stopped. After this there were upsurges of protests around the wars in Iraq and against the power of nonrepresentative global organizations like the WTO, then Arab Spring and Occupy Wall Street, then Black Lives Matter. Each time it felt to me as if everything was going to be different, the world was going to change, and every time the upsurge that flowed so powerfully eventually ebbed. But each tide left some change in its wake, and I know that it will flow again.

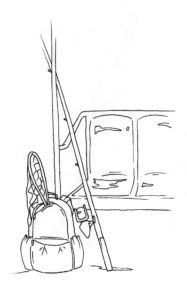

Fish Where You Are

I t's tempting to practice activism at political flashpoints: the big demonstrations at global economic summits and the sites of popular unrest around the country. This is where the action is, and you and your issue are guaranteed media coverage. Over the years I've watched fellow activists hop from one hotspot to another, acting and organizing where and when the time is right and then moving on when it's not. I'm guilty of a version of this activist tourism myself. Although I was never a "crisis hopper," for the past decade I've traveled around the world training local activists working on their local issues — from government corruption to health care access to, once, Scottish Independence — staying for a week or so, contributing as much and as best as I can, and then jetting off to the next locale and issue. This sort of touristic engagement feeds the action cravings that most activists, including myself, have, and local activists often, though not always, appreciate the additional resources and perspectives that outsiders bring with them. Sometimes this concentration of talent, resources, and attention can have a momentous impact; I'm reminded of MLK and the Southern Christian Leadership Conference's famous campaign to desegregate Birmingham, Alabama in 1963. But social change happens and, more importantly, is sustained through long-term efforts and deep relationships that establish the firm foundations necessary to challenge old institutions and build new ones. While the big, flashy activist actions get a lot of attention and press, small actions, close to home, matter more and their impact lasts longer. Activism begins at home. Yet, social change can still happen on a global scale because every place is home to someone.

After a long, dry summer, the big stripers are biting like crazy off the ocean beaches in Cape Cod and bluefish are schooling in the bay and fattening up for winter. And I am back in New York City hearing all this from my weekly YouTube fishing report from Cape Cod. School is in session, I am teaching in-person, papers need to be graded, my calendar is filled up with meetings, and I simply can't justify making the five hour drive out to the Cape. So, instead, I get up early on Saturday morning, pack up my collapsible rod, and take the subway uptown. I get out of the station at the Museum of Natural History, buy a watery coffee from a sidewalk cart, and head into Central Park where I fish for thoroughly urbanized carp and catfish with supermarket frozen corn and balls of processed bread in a man-made lake. The water's not very beautiful: plastic bags and other garbage wash around in the murky algae-covered water at my feet, and I can't eat the fish I catch; not only is it illegal, but fish fed on bread and plastic won't be very tasty. But this artificial lake in the middle of Manhattan is where I can fish right now.

Wonder Bread

As far as I can tell, nearly the entire ecosystem of Central Park's lakes lives on bread. The ducks, mallards, geese, and swans eat it. The red-eared slider and painted and box turtles eat it. And the sunfish, catfish, and carp eat it too. They do not eat just any bread. They don't crave my dense all-rye sourdough Danish Rugbrød with its whole pumpkin, sunflower, and flax seed that I am — justifiably, in my opinion — famous amongst my neighbors for baking. No, the birds, reptiles, and fish of Central Park's waterways prefer white bread, the softer the better, with over-processed, additive-enriched Wonder Bread being their favorite. This strange food dependency began, of course, with humans who, despite the many signs forbidding it, toss bread out onto the water to attract the cute ducks and turtles. The bread they miss then slips underwater and further down the food chain. Processed white bread cannot be good for the fish — it certainly isn't good for humans — and I feel a twinge of guilt that I am contributing to this destructive mono diet by using it to tempt a bite. I've tried fishing with other baits and lures, but if it's carp, catfish, or sunnies I'm after, I always resort to white bread. An unintended consequence of these fish's diet is that it's changed my own. I usually have a loaf of what our kids call "carp bread" around the kitchen, and I am regularly pressed into service by my sons into making toasted cheese sandwiches for lunch on Sundays with Wonder Bread and processed American cheese. I know they're not good for us, but damn, they taste good.

Purity is a problem for many activists. Reacting against the compromised world we are trying to change, activists create an idea of the uncompromised individual we would like to be, and then expect others around us to conform to this ideal. We tell them to eat the way we do (go vegan), dress the way we do (no logos), and talk the way we do (the ever-changing lexicon of political correctness). Having gone through this politics of purity twice, first as a punk rocker, the second time around as an activist, I am intimately familiar with the consequences. In each instance, I tried my best to purify myself of the sins of society, and every time my purity set me apart from other people — except those few who shared my views. This wasn't a problem when I was content to live as a punk in a bohemian ghetto, but as an activist trying to change the world, I discovered I was largely cut off from the people in the world I was trying to change. And this *was* a problem. As the great Detroit activist Grace Lee Boggs once said, "You cannot change any society . . . unless you see yourself as belonging to it." Over time, I learned I needed to let go of my purity in order to belong to an impure society. I also rediscovered a lot to like in things that aren't so pure — like fishing, for instance. When my friend, the activist and writer Maz Ali, heard I was writing a book on fishing and activism he wrote to me, congratulating me on this bold strategic move to engage and win over an unlikely audience by appealing to their affinities. Is that what this book is? A strategy of engagement to reach apolitical anglers and convert them to my cause? Or is it the authentic expression of my re-found love for fishing and its connections to my long-loved activism? I really couldn't tell you, because for an experienced activist the lines between strategy and authenticity are never that clear.

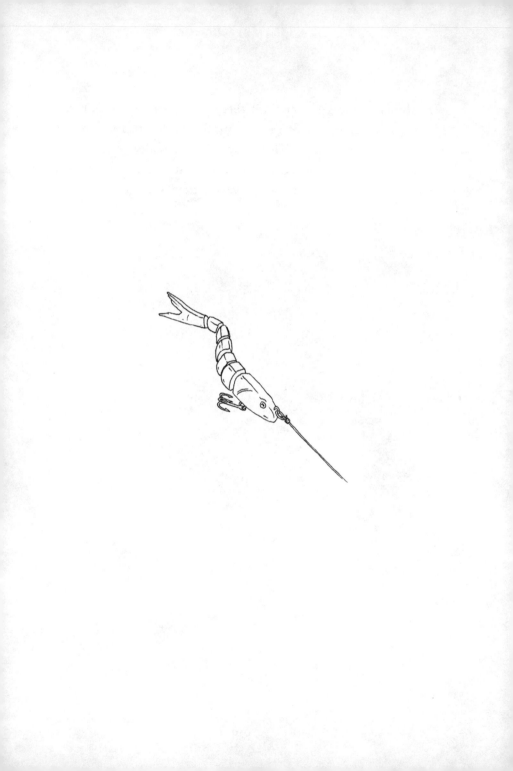

Testing Tackle

When I get a new lure I like to test it out in shallow, clear water. I study how it moves: what happens when I reel in fast or slow, the motions it makes when I jerk it and then let it rest. Sometimes I just like to see how it falls through the water on its way to the bottom. Certain rubber worms, Gary Yamamoto's for instance, do a little wiggle on the way down that the freshwater bass in my local pond seem to find irresistible. But I don't expect to catch fish when I'm testing out a lure, in fact, the expectation that I might catch fish gets in the way of the testing. In search of a bite, I'll find myself casting out to a spot far out in the pond where I just saw a fish rise and where I have no hope of seeing how my lure is performing. The same holds for testing new (or in my case, usually very old) rods and reels. It takes time to understand the particularities of the gear and to adapt my techniques in order to use the rod and reel to its best advantage. Rushing into the business of catching fish, in my experience, usually results in bad casts, snarled lines, parts lost in the water, and missed fish. Most of all, it results in a lot of frustration. Once I've tested out my tackle, understand how it works, and know what it's good and not good for, am I then ready to catch fish.

Too often, activists don't test out their tactics. At best, we plan the logistics and map out the scenario for weeks or even months, hold endless meetings to decide what words go into the pamphlet and how confrontational to be with the police, and then we leave our meeting spaces for the streets and hold our protest. At worst we do almost no planning and just go out to do it anyway. Either way, the action only happens once in the whole process and then only at the very end. It shouldn't be this way. Some time ago, in an old copy of *Life* magazine, I came across a photo series of Civil Rights activists taking part in lunch counter sit-ins in the early 1960s. The pictures are not the famous ones we usually see of jeering bigots pouring abuse on protesters sitting peacefully at a lunch counter. Instead, these pictures occur *before* that event. In one picture, in what looks like a college classroom, a student blows smoke straight into another's face as she sits impassively at a desk. In the next, a would-be activist has hot coffee spilled on him. What were these young activists doing? They were rehearsing, practicing for what was likely to happen when they sat down at a whites-only lunch counter to protest segregation. There's an enduring myth that Civil Rights activists were simply people of conviction and courage who one day had enough and spontaneously decided to take a stand. Nothing could be further from the truth. They had conviction and courage, yes, but they trained, they rehearsed, they staged the same actions over and over again and reflected on what worked and what didn't, and then they did them again. Training activists today, we encourage this sort of practicing and testing. We ask people to rehearse their actions in front of a public — even if that "public" is only family and friends — when nothing is at stake. Testing out the action in this way prepares the activists for how they might react, and also provides a sense of how an audience might respond, both of which help them refine their technique. Only having tested activism in the shallows are we then ready to move into deeper waters.

Every Fish Is a Picture

Last Saturday I was fishing in my favorite place at Central Park Lake, on the downside of a rocky outcropping that juts out into the water. After weeks of trial and error, I had perfected the ideal bait for the huge bread-eating carp that populate the lake. I threaded a long-shank hook through a hard crust of day-old baguette for buoyancy and packed a ball of Wonder Bread around the bend to hide the hook, lend some weight, and dissolve slowly underwater. Watching for the swirl in the water that signaled a carp underneath I cast out and almost immediately got a hit. My rod doubled and my drag squealed as the powerful fish pulled the line off my reel and headed for the middle of the lake. I played the fish carefully and reeled in slowly. In compliance with the park's catch-and-release rules, I had pinched the barb off my hook to make the fish easier to release, but without a barb it's a challenge to keep a thrashing, spinning fish on the hook when reeling it in. After fifteen minutes of epic struggle, I got the nearly yard-long, bewhiskered and golden-scaled, primeval-looking beast to shore. Wanting to prove to my disbelieving friends that there are, in fact, fish in Central Park and I was, in fact, catching them, I searched in the pocket of my jeans for my smartphone to take a picture. As I was pulling out my phone, being extra careful so as to not drop it into the water, I released just enough pressure on the line for the fish to do one final flip, slip my hook, and head back into the lake. My friends still don't quite believe I catch fish in Central Park.

David Solnit once said to me, "You have to think of your protest as a picture, because that's how most people will see it." David knows what he's talking about. As one of the leaders of the creative activist group Art and Revolution, he was largely responsible for the look and feel of the anti-WTO protests in 1999, and partly responsible for turning "The Battle for Seattle" into a worldwide media image (the overreaction of the Seattle riot police was also helpful in this regard). The experience of being in a protest is profound; it's a visceral feeling of solidarity and power as masses of people, just like you, take over a street for a common cause. But most people will experience a protest only through pictures in a newspaper, on TV, or through social media. This was something recognized early, and brilliantly, by the US Civil Rights movement. Events such as Rosa Parks refusing to give up her seat on a bus, peaceful students set upon by racist mobs while sitting at lunch counters, and children being marched off to jail were choreographed with as much thought and precision as a movie production. In our training, we encourage activists to see their actions as an image. When brainstorming new tactics, we ask them to physically act out their intervention ideas and then freeze in a tableau in order to get a sense of the picture the protest will convey. Thinking of protest as a picture is a good activist practice. Yet, equally important is to not get so concerned about looking good and creating an image of your protest that the reasons for protesting are overlooked. Challenging and changing power is what's important, and a good picture is only good if it accomplishes this.

Favorite Spots and New Spots

Sunday morning, just as the sun is coming up, I pull my rental bike out of its rack, secure my gear in the front basket, and ride through largely empty Greenwich Village streets, watching a few COVID-heedless partygoers stagger home on the sidewalk and swerving to avoid a pair of fearless pigeons in the middle of the road pecking at a pizza crust discarded the night before. Turning uptown on the bike lane at 6th Avenue, I pedal past Macy's, then Bryant Park, through Times Square and past Radio City Music Hall until I hit the lush green boundary of Central Park at 59th Street. I follow the park's western edge up, past the monumental facades of the churches and synagogues of the well-heeled and their secular equivalents: the Ethical Culture Society, the New York Historical Society, and finally the Museum of Natural History, where I dock my bike, get off, and enter the park. After a short walk on a paved path through the Ramble, I step over a low fence and wind my way through the woods to the water's edge, and I am finally there. My favorite spot. Like all anglers, I have my favorite places where I spend a lot of time fishing. This one, on a boulder jutting out into the lake, lets me cast out in three directions and puts me high enough above the water that I can see the fish rising to the surface. It's quiet and secluded, surrounded by oaks and maples, and offers a beautiful vista of the lake, the park beyond and, in the distance, towering skyscrapers. But as much as I love my spot, I am not wed to it. I always have an eye out for new spots: the overhanging trees on the opposite side of the lake, for instance, which seems like a shady, cool place for fish to hang out in the heat of the day. Every once in a while, I leave the safety and comfort of my usual haunts and try out one of these new spots. Sometimes for an hour, sometimes for an afternoon. If nothing is biting, then I'll go back to my old spot, nothing lost but an hour or an afternoon. If I do catch fish then I've found what might become a new favorite spot.

There are activist tactics that have always worked. One of my first activist jobs was for an outfit known and respected for their logistical abilities in pulling off mass marches in the US capital. Such demonstrations had been a mainstay of protest since the Civil Rights and Anti-War Movements, and the annual March on Washington was a tried-and-true formula to draw attention to an issue and flex a little political muscle. But by the time I had joined "the movement" in the 1980s, marches were getting a bit tired and stale. I tried out other modes of activism: ACT UP's media zaps and the street-protest-cum-rave parties of Reclaim the Streets. I went on to train activists in "artistic" forms of activism: comic street performances and eye-catching visual spectacles. These new types of activism seemed to work better, garner more media attention, and were certainly more fun than those tired and tiring marches. There were also plenty of new tactics I tried that didn't work so well (I've come to despise flash mobs: heavy on spectacle, light on message). What mattered most was that I — and hundreds of thousands of other activists — were willing to try new tactics in new settings.

Without this spirit of exploration, the novel occupations of public squares that swept the globe in 2011, from Arab Spring to Occupy Wall Street, would never have happened. Sometimes, however, bygone tactics are worth returning to. In the summer of 2020, as people across the US took to the streets demanding that Black Lives Matter and the country has reluctantly begun to acknowledge its legacy of white supremacy, I'm reminded that old favorites like mass marches can still deliver the goods.

Fishing with the Family Dog

Our family dog Simon, a normally calm and sweet Labrador Retriever, is a terrible fishing companion. I found this out one day when I thought it would be fun to take him with me as I fished for schoolies off my jetty. In my mind's eye, Simon would sit there serenely, looking up at me with his deep brown eyes, and perhaps let out an excited but mild yip in admiration when I hauled in a fish. A scene that Norman Rockwell might have painted for the cover of *Field & Stream*. Instead, Simon barked loudly and incessantly from the moment we arrived on the jetty. As I tried to cast, he jumped up on me, lunging at the barbed lure on the end of my line. Watching the lure hit the water, he scrambled down the rocky embankment in an effort to retrieve it, then fell into the current and had to be pulled back onto dry land. Shaking himself off, he barked some more. After thirty minutes of this, I gave up, ended my fishing, and brought him home. I am disappointed that Simon is not the fishing friend I dreamed of, but there's plenty of ways we still find companionship: we go on long walks in the woods and on the beach, we hang out on the deck and keep guard over our chickens, we snuggle together on the couch in front of the fireplace when it's cold. There's a whole lot we can do together; we just can't go fishing.

Politics, specifically progressive activist politics, make up a large part of my life. Not only as an activity, but in terms of identity: it's who I am, through and through. There's nothing I like more than hanging out with my friends, drinking a few beers, complaining how crazy the Republicans have become and how lame the Democrats have always been, talking strategy and devising tactics, and imagining what we would do if we ran things. These friends are diverse in terms of where they live and what they do, their nationality, ethnicity, gender and sexuality, but they all share my political views and my activist practice. I also have friends and acquaintances who do not. A lot of them are friends from high school who I've remained close to. Some are neighbors, others are regulars from the dog run or a fishing spot, one is a barber I've been going to see for the past twenty years. With these friends, I don't talk politics, especially not now in these highly partisan times. I call them out if they say something bigoted, or repeat some stupid "fact" they've pulled off a conspiracy site, but most of the time I steer the conversation to things we do share: memories, kids and dogs, the weather, a backyard fence, and whether the fish are biting. Perhaps this avoidance is cowardice on my part, but it allows me to enjoy these folks as friends. It seems like a paradox, but I believe that having friends whom I *cannot* talk to about my progressive activism makes me a better progressive activist. Activism is not about hanging out with people who already agree with you, it's about understanding and reaching those who don't.

Fishing for Connection

I am out fishing at sunrise on the Christopher Street Pier. It's a misty, cold morning and after a few minutes one of the elderly Chinese men who frequently fish there shows up. Recognizing that I am encroaching on his usual space, I nod in his direction and move over to give him room at the railing. Then we stand, fifteen feet apart, watching our propped-up poles for the telltale dip that means a fish is nibbling. Neither of us are having much luck, but I am having a little more than him so he walks over and asks me what bait I am using. I tell him it's shrimp and launch into an overly detailed story about being out of other bait and then discovering the shrimp in a bag in the bottom of my freezer left over from a Moqueca, a Brazilian shrimp and fish stew, I cooked months ago. But given his limited understanding of English, and my absolute ignorance of Cantonese, I'm pretty sure I lose him, so I simply hand him a few frozen shrimp. He nods his thanks, and we both go back to our fishing. The mist has turned into a steady drizzle and we are both standing back from our rods taking advantage of the cover of the pavilion that stands at the end of the pier. Periodically, I run out to my rod and check the line to feel for nibbling. After the third or fourth time, my fellow angler comes over to me with a little bell that attaches to the tip of my pole and tinkles if a fish is on the line. I nod my thanks, attach it to the end of my rod, and we both go back to fishing. By 8 a.m., I'm cold and it's time to go to work so I wind up my bait, break apart my rod, pack up my gear, and head over to the old man to hand him back his bell. He smiles and gestures that it's mine to keep, and we nod to one another in a small moment of shared human connection. Lately, in these days of divisiveness, most of my cross-class, many of my cross-ethnicity, and nearly all of my cross-political exchanges have taken place while fishing or discussing fishing.

Paul's letters in the New Testament of The Bible should be up there with Saul Alinsky's *Rules for Radicals* as required reading for every activist. As much as I despise the Apostle Paul for what he did to Jesus's teachings by turning love and forgiveness into rules and intolerance, I have to admire his skill as an organizer in turning a ragtag bunch of rebels into the nascent Christian Church. Here he is dispensing invaluable activist advice in 1 Corinthians:

> Though I am free and belong to no one, I have made myself a slave to everyone, to win as many as possible. To the Jews I became like a Jew, to win the Jews . . . To the weak I became weak, to win the weak. I have become all things to all people so that by all possible means I might save some.

Paul may have been a shameless opportunist, but he also understood that in order to reach people, to connect with people, and to convert people you need to be able to meet them where they are. Too often activists don't do this. We insist on meeting people where *we* are, or where we would like *them to be*. This may work amongst the already converted, but to bring about broad social change we need to connect with those who don't know, don't care, or don't agree with us (aka the infidels). To create these connections requires recognizing and nurturing commonalities. This doesn't mean pretending to be who you are not, it means finding what we share with others and starting there: being a mother, a son, or a devoted partner; an avid gardener, lover of romantic comedies, a pop music fan, or, yes, an angler.

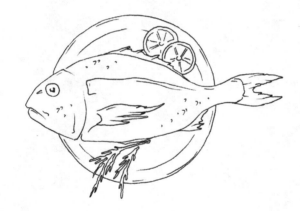

A Good Day

The anglers I fish alongside on the Christopher Street Pier approach fishing differently than I do. They arrive with multiple poles, all of them heavy power, which they line up across the side railing with little bells on top that tingle when a fish gets hooked. Their reels are loaded with high pound test monofilament, and often even higher test braided line, so they can safely haul the fish up to the pier from the water fifteen feet below. For bait they favor small, live crab, the favorite food of the Tautogs we are all hoping to catch. I, however, fish with light tackle and line, usually only one rod, and bait my hooks with leftover frozen shrimp. We take different approaches because we are after different things. The other anglers do what they do because they are fishing for food for themselves and their families, or maybe to sell to a local fish market. Success means catching and landing a lot of fish. I, on the other hand, am fishing for the excitement of sensing the hit when a fish takes the bait and then struggling to bring the fish in, and I don't eat what I catch. (I give my fish to my fellow anglers who, in turn, supply me with crabs for bait when I run out of shrimp. We seem to have come to a tacit agreement that I now work for them.) For all our differences, there is also a lot we share: grumbling when the tide is running too fast and our rigs get swept out, posing for phone photos with a big catch, and, of course, the tedious wait for a bite. But because what we are after is different, what we consider a good day of fishing differs too.

Since I work with activists to make them better activists, I think a lot about what defines good activism. Tapping into my academic training as a social scientist, I've even developed assessment models in the past few years to determine, as objectively as possible, what constitutes success. When I first began evaluating activism, I was pretty dogmatic: activism that achieved concrete, capital-P political objectives like changing public opinion, enacting a policy, or electing a politician was good, and anything that didn't was bad. It didn't hurt that such clear and demonstrable goals made success or failure relatively easy to measure. However, by working with a lot of activists and artists who don't think like me, I've been taught to recognize other, often more internal and invisible, markers of activist success: things like instilling confidence in individuals, building community within a group, or enabling the capacity to dream. This is why my assessment practice has moved from pronouncements to questions. I start by asking: What do you want to have happen? With this answered, I move on to: How will you know if this happens? Then, after the action: What actually happened? And since activism is all about the process, not just the event, we finally address the most important question of all: Knowing what you know now, what would you do differently next time? The most important thing I've learned is that any assessment of activism always needs to take into account the intent of the activist, and what is "good" depends upon what one is after.

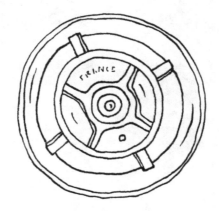

Setting Your Drag

My favorite fresh water fishing spot on Cape Cod is a small kettle pond not far from my cottage. Like all the kettle ponds on the Cape, it was created 18,000 years ago when retreating glaciers left huge ice blocks buried in the sandy soil. As the ice melted it created "kettles" that filled with soft, clean water from the water table below. Forests of maples, oaks, birch trees, and the scraggly pine trees particular to this area grew up around these kettles and created idyllic oases of plant and animal life. At some time in this millennia-long history, small and largemouth bass found their way into the ponds — and now I was doing my best to pull them back out. Using a pumpkin-green rubber worm with a chartreuse tail rigged Texas-style without a weight, I was consistently catching and landing nice size bass. Then I started hooking the monsters from the middle of the pond . . . and just as quickly lost them as they thrashed, leapt, ran for the deep, and snapped my line. One day, as I am fighting what I can only assume is the biggest bass in the entire lake, a fellow angler yells out across the pond, "Loosen your drag!" At that moment I realize that all this time I had the drag on my reel tightened down so hard that there was no give whatsoever. When an eight-pound bass took a run, it was a simple matter of physics that my six-pound test line would snap. I quickly reach down to let off the drag and my line starts screaming out, yard after yard spooling off my reel. When the fish stops running, I quickly reel the line back in. This goes on for the next ten minutes: run and reel, over and over, tightening the drag here, loosening it there, until the fish — and I — are tired and I can safely land my monster bass. There are many factors involved in setting the proper drag: the strength of your line and whether the fish has a soft or hard mouth, but that day I learn a very important lesson about resistance: you set your drag too high and you'll snap your line, but if you set it too low the fish will take it all and you'll be left with an empty reel. You always need to be adjusting your drag.

Activists, young activists in particular, can be uncompromising. The only victory is total victory and unless your adversary capitulates to your every demand the campaign is a loss. Consequently, uncompromising activists chalk up a lot of losses. Mainstream political operatives, particularly moderate ones, do the opposite: they give away everything at the first sign of resistance and are left with nothing at the end. The trick to being an effective activist is to gauge how much resistance you need to apply to get the result you need. Give your adversary too much line and you'll give away all your power. Don't give an inch and they'll dig in their heels. This calculation depends upon your strength, and it depends on your adversary. Potential allies need a little room to play and unyielding enemies need to be met with maximum resistance. As I wrote these words, the current US President, who lost both the electoral and popular vote, was making baseless claims about stolen elections and demanding that the vote go his way. His opponents, who in elections past have been prone to capitulate at the first sign, decided not to give an inch. It's the right amount of resistance. The ex-president may have a thin skin but he has a hard mouth.

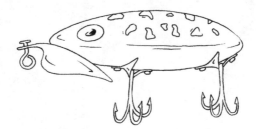

Breaking Tradition

One of my favorite activist photographs is of a young Muslim woman wearing a hijab and a T-shirt that reads: "This is what a Feminist looks like." The image reminds me that we shouldn't get hung up on the way things once were, but instead look to how things are now. Activists need to be willing to break traditions, not just with old tactics — as I've written about before — but with old ideas about activist identity. What makes an activist is always changing and the history of feminism(s) in the US is a good example of this. In the first wave of feminism, at the turn of the last century, activists drew upon patriarchal notions of "true womanhood" in a strategic move to make their case for voting rights. Dressing all in white, waving American flags, and sometimes pushing baby carriages, Suffragettes staged massive marches, rallies, and other spectacles to show their strength and refute the anti-feminist imagery of feminists as "mannish." Fast forward a half-century, and second-wave feminists were protesting against this image of domestic womanhood by throwing mops, lipstick, and high heels into a "Freedom Trash Can" at a Miss America pageant. (Alas, no bras, no fire: bra-burning, it turns out, is largely a myth.) A few years later, lesbian and feminists of color challenged "universalist" notions of women's liberation as cultural, racially, and sexually specific, and made the case for what we now call intersectional politics. In more recent times, third-wave feminists rejected what they perceived as the overly censorious culture of feminism and reappropriated lipstick and girly dresses, and yes, hijabs. Through all these permutations, the call for respect and power remains the same, but what these demands sound like, and what the people making these demands look like, have changed. It's the willingness to break tradition that's one of the reasons why feminist activism is still so active when other activisms can seem stuck in the past.

It's Thanksgiving and I've returned to fish for bass in the pond where I fished all summer. When the days were hot and the water was warm, I was killing it with my green-and-yellow rubber worm. Today, with the same lure, I get nothing. For an hour and a half, I work the shoreline, fishing in all my favorite spots: the old felled tree that lies semi-submerged off to the right, the "bass hole" (so named by a visiting 14 year old) defined by a half-moon bay off to the left, and . . . nothing. Looking at my watch, I realize I have only thirty minutes until I'm due back at home to make lunch for the boys, so I tie on a froggy-looking "jitterbug" topwater lure that I've never caught anything with. Three casts in and I have a sixteen-inch largemouth bass on my hook. It seems paradoxical, but fishing is both tediously constant (cast, retrieve, repeat) and always changing. As the weather varies, the tides shift, and the seasons change, where you've been fishing and what you've been using to catch the fish no longer work. The fish are somewhere else, or they are attracted to something else. You can keep on doing what you've been doing before, but you probably won't catch much. Or you can break tradition, adapt to the changed conditions, and try something new. You'll likely have to try many new somethings before finding a new tradition, but it's worth the disruption, uncertainty, and experimentation once you start catching fish again.

Catch and Release

Almost all the fish I catch I release back into the water. I do this for a number of reasons: the saltwater bass I catch in the sea never seem to fit into the twenty-eight to thirty-five-inch "keeper" slot allowed in Massachusetts, the freshwater bass I catch in the ponds taste like mud and stink up the kitchen if you cook them, and by law all fish caught in New York City parks have to be released, which is not much of a sacrifice as I don't relish eating a fish whose main diet consists of white bread anyway. But mainly, I choose to catch and release because my love for fishing comes from the act of fishing itself. Every once in a while, I will decide to keep and eat a fish, mainly the tasty lake trout I catch in early spring before the water heats up and drives them into the shallows or the bluefish of late summer whose oily meat is just perfect for smoking. But pan-fried trout and home-smoked bluefish are special treats, and most of the fish I eat comes from the store. The commercial fisherman of Cape Cod who supply my store-bought fish, the older Chinese men on the pier next to me who fish the Hudson River for dinner, and the Nez Perce, Umatilla, Yakama, and Warm Springs peoples who have to continually fight to keep their tribal fishing rights on the Columbia River in Washington State where my parents retired don't throw back their fish, they keep what they catch.

We open our training workshops by asking people to tell the rest of the group how they got involved in activism. Having done this with thousands of activists, around the world, I've learned that each person has their own unique story, but their stories, as different as they are, share several traits: they are experiential, they are emotional, and they are personal. In sum: they are *affective* experiences; the very sorts of experiences we hope to generate through an artistic approach to activism. I often begin this exercise using myself as an example. I grew up in an activist family with a social justice minister for a father, but I was an alienated and angry kid and my father's style of Christian activism didn't speak to me. Then, sometime in the late 1970s, I heard something that did: "Don't know what I want. But I know how to get it . . . I wanna be anarchy." It was the Sex Pistols' punk rock anthem "Anarchy in the UK." While I couldn't quite make out the words they were singing, and a lot of the references were foreign to me, I knew they, like me, were angry at the world and they wanted to change (or destroy) it. That was the moment I chose to become an activist. Once, when we were doing this exercise with a group of sex worker activists in South Africa, the next person in the circle stood up and told her story of activist awakening. "I'm poor, black, and queer; I'm a woman and a sex worker," Ruvimbo Tenga explained. "There has never been a moment when I was not an activist." I realized then, and have realized many times since then, that activism for me is a choice, while for her, and for many of the activists I work with, it is not. I can always walk away from activism, with a bad conscience, perhaps, but no deleterious impact on my life (indeed, my career prospects would likely improve). Ruvi cannot. For her, and many like her, activism is survival.

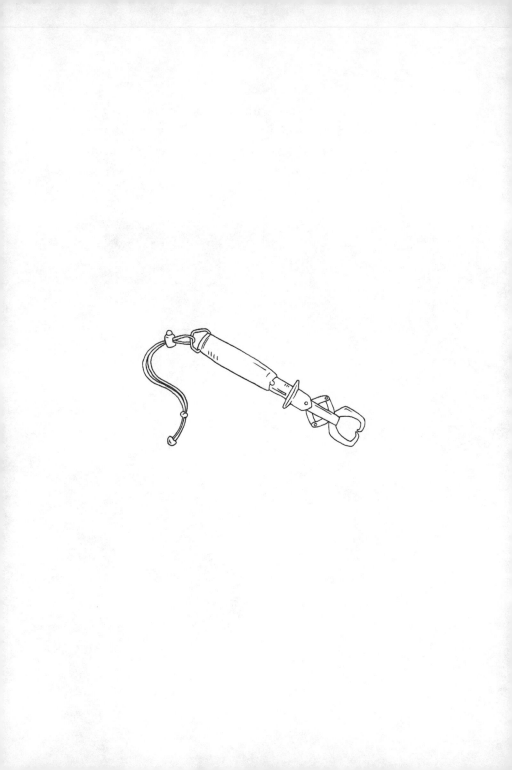

Gear

I was in Washington Square Park not long ago sharing a coffee and a catch-up with a scholar who writes and teaches on social movements and radical theory. They asked me the required question that scholars ask one another when they meet: "What are you working on now?" I knew better than to tell them I'd been working a lot on my fishing, so I described my current book project on assessing the impact of artistic activism. "That's good," they said, "because you've been kind of coasting since your last book." For the past dozen years, I had been busy working on scores of campaigns with thousands of activists around the world while holding down a full-time teaching gig. Coasting? I was exhausted. I was also angry; angry that someone who I thought shared the same commitment to radical social change could overlook the work I'd been doing to bring about that change. Then it hit me. Radicalism for this radical wasn't activism and organizing, it was primarily a set of academic ideas and lifestyle practices. And in this way, I had failed; I hadn't published an "important" book in more than a decade and I was living a middle-class life, married with two kids and a dog (a pure bred Lab to make it worse). For all our ostensible shared revolutionary desires, we don't really share much at all. Since that day they've texted me a couple of times to see if I want to get coffee and catch-up. I'm too busy to reply.

I had missed daybreak but it was still early morning when I pulled into the beach parking lot next to a large SUV with Rhode Island plates. Four guys, all in their late 20s or early 30s, were unloading their gear. It was impressive gear: top of the line St. Croix rods and Van Staal reels. They were outfitted in bib waders and surf boots with fancy tackle bags slung over their shoulders. But what caught my eye was a device hanging from one of their belts: a stainless-steel metal tube with a two fingered claw on the end that reminded me of a prosthetic robot arm from one of the science-fiction TV shows I used to watch as a kid. (I later found out it is a device used for gripping a fish's lip and weighing them at the same time, which, I've got to admit, is pretty cool.) We did what anglers do when meeting one another: wish each other luck and solicit advice on where best to fish — which I gave freely, if not entirely candidly. They clunked their way across the lot and to the beach in all their gear as I got my rods out of my rusty Jeep, slung the old Strand Bookstore bag I used to carry my surf plugs over my shoulder, slipped on my rotting canvas sneakers, and followed them. The fish weren't biting that morning, and after an hour or so I saw them leave. They didn't seem disappointed at all, and I began to think that maybe fishing for them was more about the road trip and the gear and not so much about catching the fish.

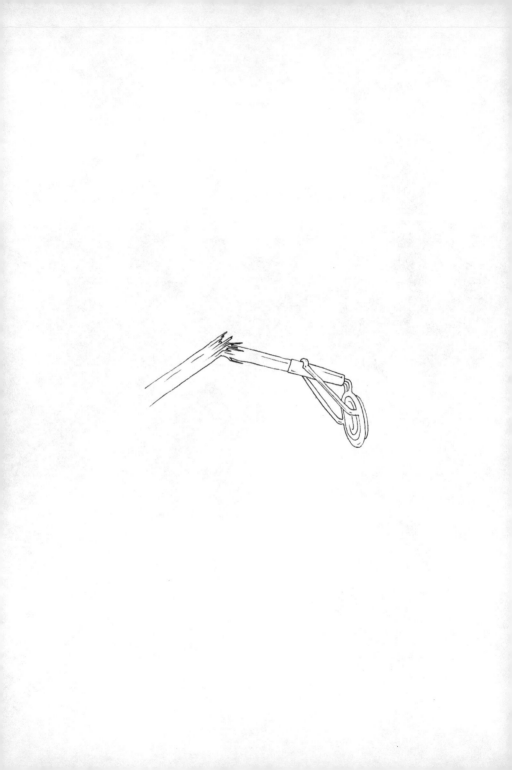

Good Days and Bad Days

As with life, so it is with fishing: you have good days and bad days. On a good day, the sun is shining, the wind is calm, my lure lands exactly where I am aiming, a hungry fish gobbles it up, and after a valiant fight (including a dramatic flip or two out of the water), I land the fish, easily unhook it, and let it swim away. And this happens again and again. That's a good day. Then there are days where everything goes wrong. The wind is up and my line snarls as I attempt to cast. It starts to rain and I discover my jacket leaks. I slip off a log and fall into the water with my phone in my pocket. And, needless to say, I don't catch any fish. On average, I have more good fishing days than bad ones and as I get to be a better angler the ratio increases in favor of the good. But I still have plenty of disappointing days catching no fish — in fact, I had one today — and every once in a while, I have a spectacularly bad day. Yet I keep fishing, because sometimes the day turns around and, if it doesn't, there's always tomorrow.

When devising tactics, we try to encourage activists to generate as many ideas for actions as possible, no matter how ridiculous or impossible they may first seem. We do this to break the tendency many activists have of settling on the first idea they come up with and putting all their efforts into it, and then getting disappointed if it doesn't work out as planned. When brainstorming a multitude of ideas, invariably, many of them are pretty bad. That's okay; in fact, it's a necessary part of the process. Steve Lambert, my frequent collaborator, has a nice way of explaining this. Think of ideas as lying around a large field. We'd like to imagine ourselves walking through that field only picking up the good ideas while leaving the bad ones behind, untouched. But that's not how it works. The process is more like the conveyor belt back in the produce processing plant, where a good idea comes after a bad one after a couple of good ones and then a few bad ones, and you have to work on them all. Sometimes a bad idea, worked upon for a while, becomes a good one. Once, we were working with veterans of the Iraq and Afghanistan wars on a campaign to extend health benefits to include coverage for moral trauma. When it came to brainstorming possible tactics, someone suggested an armed takeover of the Veterans Administration. It was a bad idea for all sorts of reasons, the least of which is we would likely all be killed. Thankfully, the violent insurrection was quickly rejected but it prompted another idea for an action. Instead of an armed takeover to force the VA to become the institution we wanted it to become, the veterans came up with the idea of creating the institution they wanted in the future right now. In the parking lot outside the real VA building, they would erect a tent, staff it with volunteer doctors and psychologists, and — for a few hours — create a VA clinic that would offer all the services they weren't getting. As a demonstration of their demands, it was a really good idea, but without the original bad idea it would never have occurred to anyone.

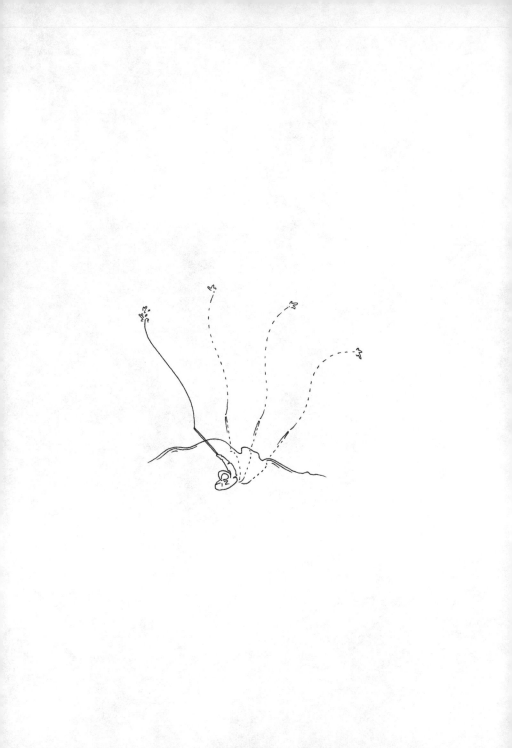

Accuracy or Coverage

When fishing for bass in my local pond, I have to make a decision: Do I cast for accuracy? Or do I cast for coverage? Casting for accuracy means being able to drop my lure exactly where I want it, like right at the edge of that branch hanging low over the water that seems like a likely place for fish to hang out. Accuracy matters because if I overshoot just a foot, my lure will wrap around the branch, get all tangled up, and I'll have to cut the line. Too short, and the fish lurking in the shade of the overhanging leaves won't notice my alluring rubber worm as it falls through the water. Casting for coverage, on the other hand, means being able to propel my worm far out into the lake where the big fish live, let it sink its way to the bottom, and then slowly retrieve it — twitching, lifting, and falling — across a maximum distance. Depending on which way I want to go, I take along a different rod and reel. For accuracy, I use a baitcaster setup: an old Abu Garcia 5000 reel and a Kunnan Competitor five-feet medium action rod with heavy braided line to pull the lure out of the brush. With its short throw, and by keeping my thumb on the spool as the line spools out, I can drop my lure on a dime (well, a dinner plate). If I want to go the distance, I use a spinning outfit: my trusty Mitchell 300 reel and seven-feet Fenwick with a light monofilament line. The longer pole, lighter line, and spinning reel lets me cast far out into the lake. A lot of the time, however, I just grab whatever rod I feel like fishing with and go to the pond and try my luck.

When thinking about audiences for actions, activists frequently, and unconsciously, default to two options: themselves or everyone. They craft their intervention to appeal only to the narrow band of people who share the same ideological concerns, common languages, and aesthetic and cultural sensibilities as themselves. Or they veer in the opposite direction, creating actions with the most general and generic of appeals in order to offend no one and include as wide a demographic as possible. The former has a specificity that makes it more likely to resonate with its target audience. But that audience is manifestly minuscule. The latter approach has the potential to break out of "preaching to the choir" and reach the mass audience that's necessary for any sort of social change. But such a mass audience is too broad, too diverse, and too massive to reach and touch with any singular appeal, so this sort of lowest common denominator approach usually appeals to no one. What works best is to locate your audience between one and one million, identifying groups of people who are large enough to make a difference, yet share enough commonalities to create an intervention that speaks directly to them and their concerns. With a lot of thought, and a bit of luck, your action lands with your audience exactly as you want it to.

Angling with Aristotle

Fishing with live bait entails a lot of watching, sensing, and waiting for a nibble. How long to wait is always a question. I've stared out across the water at my bobber, watching it do nothing, only to come to the conclusion after a fruitless hour that there are absolutely no fish where I've cast and I've just been wasting my time. On the other hand, I've also had days where I get impatient, casting out bait only to let it sit for only a couple of minutes before hauling it in again, never giving a curious fish a chance to find it. Deciding whether to do nothing or do something, and when the right time is for each, extends throughout fishing. Once you see your bobber dunk under, or feel a pull on your line, you need to set the hook in order to catch the fish. If you yank back on your pole too soon, too hard, you'll end up with half-eaten bait and no fish on the line. But if you wait too long, there's a good chance that the wily fish will carefully strip your hook and swim away. Perhaps Aristotle was thinking of fishing when he came up with his concept of the golden mean, finding a happy place between "excess" and "deficiency," between too much and too little.

Sometimes waiting is essential with activism: waiting for an event that thrusts your issue into the limelight, the moment when your opponent slips up, or when public opinion swings your way. But sometimes waiting around is the wrong move, and you need to force the action. When we first formed our community activist group in the Lower East Side, we decided that our first campaign was going to focus on government complicity in gentrification. I remember a more experienced member, Alex Vitale, lobbying for an action immediately. I argued we weren't ready, we needed to research and discuss the issue more amongst ourselves, devise a strategy and objectives and then, and only then, would we be ready to do an action. "It's true we aren't ready," Alex replied, "but if we don't take action now, we will be one of those activist groups who talk about acting but don't actually do it." We did the action: a banner drop in front of the local Housing and Urban Development office calling out the state-sanctioned practice of warehousing empty apartments. The banner tangled in the scaffolding and our message couldn't be read, which really didn't matter because no one from the community or the press showed up to read it. I was right: we weren't ready to act and the action was terrible. Yet, Alex was also right: that action moved us from a talking group to an action group and set the stage for much more successful, well-attended, and well-covered events in future months. Maybe Aristotle was wrong: it's not so much finding a place between doing nothing and doing too much, it's knowing that each has its own value, at its own time.

Cleaning Up Hooks and Lures

"Whose streets? Our streets!" It's a classic activist refrain, and one I've chanted thousands of times in thousands of marches. It's a statement of power and agency: using our bodies and voices to take over a public street as the authorities try to keep us on the sidewalks, and in line. Yet, it's not only "our" streets, nor are they "their" streets — they are streets shared with everyday people. I remember once doing a training action with a group of activists in a market area in the capital city of Bosnia-Herzegovina, Sarajevo. The first thing the activists did when we arrived on the scene was to visit all the shopkeepers in the surrounding area to let them know who they were (activists from the Western Balkans); what they were doing (a street theater protest); how long they would be doing it (two hours); and why they were doing it (to protest governmental corruption). They did not ask the shopkeepers for their permission but, as one of them explained later. "We are coming into their space, where they live and work, and since we are going to cause a disruption it is a simple matter of respect to let them know what was going on." (This consideration was not extended to the police or authorities, who were not informed as they would have shut down the action immediately.) Not everyone they talked to was happy, nor did everyone approve of the political message we were trying to convey in the performance, but they did appreciate the gesture of respect and as the activists performed their action, I noticed several locals coming out from behind their shop doors to watch, smile, and nod their heads in agreement.

Fishing, particularly freshwater fishing, means snagging. I cast too close to the log sticking out into the water, under which I just know fish are lurking, and my line gets wrapped around it. Or I cast into overhead branches or get hooked on an underwater obstruction. I pull my line, try a couple of different angles, and pull again, but sometimes, most of the time, the snag just won't get unsnagged and I need to cut my line. Looking around, I see I'm not the only one. Hanging from trees, or tracing lines below water, I spot cut lines from other anglers. At the end of the fishing season, the shoreline is just littered with the stuff. These left behind lines and lures aren't just ugly — they're dangerous. Old ladies swim the circumference of my favorite pond for their morning exercise, kids splash in the shallows, and the water and shoreline are home to birds, turtles and, of course, fish — all of whom can get tangled in the line and stabbed by the hooks. So, every once in a while, wearing swim trunks in the summer and chest-high waterproof waders in spring and fall, I wade out to the weed beds and jutting logs and clean up the mess. Sometimes I find still-serviceable lures that I clean up and add to my collection (a plastic froggy bait I found has become one of my favorites), but most of the time it's just yards of line and rusted hooks. This simple stewardship reminds me that "my" favorite fishing spots aren't really mine; they're something we all share.

Bright Red Blood

Revealing my passion for fishing to fellow progressives generates a set number of responses. Sometimes, it's one of enthusiastic surprise and a story of how some significant person in their life loved fishing or a conspiratorial and somewhat guilty admission that they, themselves, secretly enjoy fishing too. More often, I'm met with confused silence as the person can't reconcile my fishing with our ostensibly shared progressive values. When this cognitive dissonance dissipates, a lecture about animal rights or the ecological ramifications of the depletion of marine life often begins. I've practiced my stock replies: sport fishers are not the ones depleting fish stocks, the problem lies with the profit-driven fish trawlers scooping up everything in their wake so we can have inexpensive frozen cod at the supermarket. If my critics aren't convinced, and they rarely are, I'll follow up with the standard hunter's response: if you enjoy eating it you should be able to stomach killing it. These arguments are fruitless against vegetarians, I know, but I try to mollify them by explaining I release most of what I catch. But for all my arguments, I have to admit, privately, that their concerns are valid: fishing is brutal. No matter how diligent I am about employing the best catch and release practices — using hooks with the barbs pinched off, never using a gaff, and relying upon silicone landing nets that won't disturb the slime that protects a trout's delicate skin — fish still get hurt.

Instead of being hooked in the tough cartilage of their lip, they swallow the hook and it gets lodged down their throat. Trying to get it out, or cutting the line and leaving the hook in, I risk mortally damaging the fish. Maybe they will heal after this trauma, or maybe they will become part of the food cycle by providing a meal for the snapping turtles or crabs, but there is no denying the fact that I have left the fish in a worse state than when I caught it. And no matter how humanely I try to kill a fish I plan to eat, whether I stun it first or sever their spinal cord or bleed the fish out by cutting the gill rakers, I still hurt it. And, as I discovered with my first kill, fish bleed bright red blood.

People get hurt in activism, no matter how concerned and careful you are. I've planned demonstrations for months, set up non-violent civil disobedience training weeks in advance, assigned skilled negotiators to liaison with the police, and then during the action one bottle gets thrown, the police charge in swinging their clubs and fists, and protestors end up bloody and in jail. Activism, if you are any good, also hurts your opponent. I recall one campaign we waged in the Lower East Side against a particularly egregious developer who was buying up an old school building that housed a beloved community center in order to turn it into a luxury apartment building. We protested, we sat-in and occupied the building, we filed legal injunctions, we picketed his suburban home, and we stopped him. It was one of those rare victories in activism. We also bankrupted his business and his employees lost their jobs. "Good," you might say, "the greedy bastard deserved it."

And he did, but we also destroyed his dream and harmed those who depended on him. If I were to do it again, I wouldn't change a thing: I'd still stage that protest and still bankrupt the developer, but I'd do it recognizing that people would get hurt, and that activism entails making moral choices and owning up to the results.

The World Is a Fish

When you have been fishing for a while you start to look at the world as a person who fishes. When I go to the beach with my wife to relax in our beach chairs, read books, and be lulled by the waves, I can't help myself from looking out past the waves for baitfish jumping. In the late afternoons on blisteringly hot days when my sons and I go to one of the kettle ponds to cool off by floating out to the middle of the pond on our inner tubes, I scan the shoreline from my new vantage point looking for promising spots to follow up on in future fishing trips. In the city, on my morning runs to the Hudson River, I always make sure to peer into the buckets of the old men fishing on the pier, making mental note of what they are catching and what bait they are using. There's an old saying that to a person with a hammer, the world is a nail. To an angler, the world is a potential fish. Like many anglers I know, I've come to keep a collapsible fishing rod and a little tackle box in the back of my car even when I am not planning on fishing . . . just in case.

Down at the bottom of the road where I live in Cape Cod, where the road gives way to an estuary, there is a path that traces the boundaries of the salt marsh, twisting and turning, all the way to the bay beach about a half-mile or so away. A neighbor tells me she has walked that path with her dog nearly every day for a half-century and that the path has existed for as long as anyone can remember. This summer, however, a tenants' association for a cluster of houses at the end of the road tried to restrict access to the path, putting up a big sign proclaiming, "Private Property." If I wasn't an activist, I'd probably get angry, mutter private threats, or, as my seventy-five-year-old neighbor has done, simply ignore the sign and continue walking her dog along the path as she has always done. Instead, I spend the day researching Massachusetts shoreline access rights. Rooted in a Colonial-era ordinance extending private property rights all the way out to the low tide mark, they are some of the worst in the country. That evening I invite a few local activist friends over to our deck for a strategy session. First, we come up with a Name and Shame campaign publicizing the ostensibly "progressive" property owners in the community who are the most egregious enforcers of this regressive law. As the number of beers drunk increase, the number and boldness of our ideas increase proportionately, and we start entertaining the possibility of more direct action against the signs restricting shoreline access that have been popping up along the shoreline. Before the night is over, we have a plan, a timeline, and tasks assigned to each of us. To an activist, the world is a place to act, and the decision to act or not act is yours; the anguish of responsibility is what the existentialist philosopher Jean-Paul Sartre called it. Looking at the world through an activist's eyes means that where others can rant or ignore, you always know something could be done, and you could be the one doing it. A few nights ago "someone" tore down the Private Property sign at the end of my road.

Angler in the Afternoon

I remember once, when I was in my twenties, sitting in a bar after an action when a woman who was part of the activist scene in the Lower East Side, but whom I didn't know very well, came up and asked me: "Do you have a lover, or are you married to The Revolution?" I think she was just being flirtatious, or at least I flatter myself in thinking so, and I don't recall what I said at the time, but I do remember thinking what an odd either/or proposition it was. Lover *or* Activist. Revealing my proclivities, perhaps a bit too much, a quote from Karl Marx now comes readily to mind:

> For as soon as the distribution of labour comes into being, each man has a particular, exclusive sphere of activity, which is forced upon him and from which he cannot escape. He is a hunter, a fisherman, a herdsman, or a critical critic, and must remain so if he does not want to lose his means of livelihood; while in communist society, where nobody has one exclusive sphere of activity but each can become accomplished in any branch he wishes, society regulates the general production and thus makes it possible for me to do one thing today and another tomorrow, to hunt in the morning, fish in the afternoon, rear cattle in the evening, criticise after dinner, just as I have a mind, without ever becoming hunter, fisherman, herdsman or critic.

The best — and happiest — activists I know are not only good activists, but also good lovers, workers, dancers, musicians, gardeners, bakers, readers, runners, and, yes, hunters, shepherds, critics, and anglers.

One of the things that makes fishing so enjoyable for me is that it is not activism. It is also not my work as a teacher or my career as an academic, nor is it being a good husband and father. When I am on the water, looking for a fish rising or a good obstruction under which some fish might be hiding, my pole in hand waiting for the quick pull that signals a fish in my line, my mind both focusses and drifts. Like in a Japanese tea ceremony I once attended, where every motion was circumscribed and ritualized, I am simultaneously completely in the moment and a million miles away. It would be easy to say that fishing is an escape from the responsibilities of my life, but that's not entirely accurate. Fishing is more a supplement; it doesn't take away from my other roles in life (though my family, comrades, and editor might disagree) but adds to them. An obvious example of this addition is the book I am writing here, but there are other complements as well. After a few hours of fishing, I am less short with my kids, more supportive of my wife, more serene at faculty meetings (daydreaming of fishing, rather than getting enraged at petty academic squabbles), and recharged enough to dive back into the anguish of the world and the activism that might change it for the better.

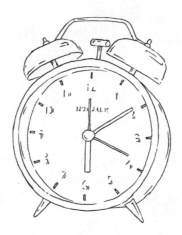

Early Worm Gets the Fish

Most people dream about sleeping in on weekends or vacations; I think about getting up early and going fishing. I set my alarm to 4:00 a.m., drag myself out of bed, brew a cup of coffee, gather my gear, and then get into my old Jeep or on the subway or a rental bike and head out to my favorite fishing spot just as the sun rises. Other anglers I know are evening people, arriving on the beach, lake, or stream just as the sun sets and then staying there, in the pitch black, when other folks are home snuggling up to watch TV or out partying on the town. There's good reason to get up early or go out late: mornings and evenings tend to be good fishing times, the water is cooler, bugs and baitfish are active, all of which means the bigger fish are biting as well. But sometimes fishing at these opportune times is impossible. I need to get the kids up early and fed and off to school with packed lunches. Or my family intervenes in the evening, insisting that sit-down dinner gets priority over a dash to the water. And so I go fishing at midday, during my lunchtime, sneaking in forty-five minutes to an hour with my rod and reel. I've learned to fish when I can, and when my schedule, commitments, sleep-cycle and energy-level allows. The fishing conditions are not always ideal, and my yield sometimes suffers, but fishing when I do have time is better than not fishing at all.

As an activist I often feel the pressure to be active all the time. There's no doubt that if activists were active all the time more activism would happen and, presumably, more social change would be the result. But there's a problem with this equation: it doesn't factor in people's lives. Being active all the time is a certain path to activist burnout. I can't tell you how many gung-ho, married-to-the-revolution activists I know who found 24-7 activism unsustainable, quit, and then retreated from politics. (I've done it myself a few times now.) This push for total commitment also limits the type of people who become activists, with the ideal profile being someone with no job, no family, and no social life outside of activism. Recognizing these problems, my community organizing comrade Leslie Kauffman came up with an idea for something we called "scalable commitment." Every flier we produced and handed out had information about our issue on one side, and on the flipside had a list of things people could do — given their time and energy. These ranged from fifteen minutes a week (usually call a local politician) to an hour a week (write letters and make posts) to a lot of time on their hands (come join us). The brilliance of this idea is that it didn't expect a full-time commitment to activism, yet gave everyone an opportunity to take meaningful action . . . how and when they could.

White Man Fishing on the Cape

As the sun rises over the beach and the sky glows purple, red, then orange, and finally turns to blue, I remind myself for the umpteenth time how fortunate I am. Not fortunate in some sort of idyllic, abstract way, but fortunate as the concrete consequence of my race, class, gender, sexuality, and geography. I am privileged. Fishing is not a particularly privileged activity. It's dominated by men, true, but it is not a rich man's sport — though fly fishing can certainly lean that way. Nor is it particularly white. My fellow anglers on the Christopher Street Pier are almost exclusively Asian, those casting their lines into Central Park's lakes with me are often Black and Latino, and any trip to an urban pier or a country brook (or all of fishing-obsessed Japan) will dispel simplistic racial stereotypes. Yet my own love for fishing is largely dependent on the fact that I have a decent salary, a flexible schedule, and can afford a mortgage on a house in Cape Cod and rent on an apartment in New York City. My fishing is untroubled by the need to work double shifts at the local Stop and Shop to make ends meet or worry about getting hassled by the police because of the color of my skin as I pull up to an empty beach parking lot after dark. Hell, I wouldn't be fishing at all if European colonizers hadn't forced the Nauset peoples off the Cape and the Lenape out of Manhattan. Recognizing my privilege doesn't keep me from enjoying fishing, but there is no escaping it: I am a White Man Fishing on the Cape.

These days, when my privilege as a white, straight, middle-class, US-born, cis-male is increasingly identified and called out by others, I find myself wondering what I should do. How can I be an effective activist against the powers-that-be when I so resemble them? I could continue on in the great white way of refusing to acknowledge that my activist experiences and ideas are colored by my privilege, and then become angry and bitter as my experience and ideas are rejected or ignored by others. Or I might conclude that my activism is so tainted by my privilege that the only right thing to do is stop being an activist, and retreat into a guilt-ridden, yet morally righteous, solipsistic inactivity. (Guilt privileges the privileged by, once again, making it all about themselves.) But neither of these choices helps bring about social change, at least not in the ways that I would like to see. The only thing I can honestly do with my privilege is to own up to it, and to use it. When I was still in college, I traveled to Nicaragua with a group of New York-based carpenters to build houses for the revolution. Camped out in an abandoned hacienda in a remote border region where anti-revolutionary guerillas were still active, constructing houses every day in the hot sun while protected by soldiers with AK-47's, it felt as if I had left my life in the United States far behind. I was now a third-world revolutionary. *Viva Sandanista!* But at some point, I realized why we were stationed in a combat zone. Our real job was to use our US bodies to deter attacks in the area by the US-funded Contra guerillas. Anybody with some rudimentary skill could swing a hammer; it was my privileged status as a US citizen that, paradoxically, made me so valuable to the revolution. Here, now, my privilege does not make me a better activist. In many ways, it makes me a worse one in that I can be blind to other's experiences. What my privilege does give me is power in the world: I can do things that for others would lead to immediate arrest or worse. I have access to resources and people in power that others don't. I have a confidence and boldness born from my position. It is important to recognize this, to be sure, but recognition alone changes nothing. I know it's my responsibility to act with and through my privilege to help build a world where privilege no longer exists.

One Last Cast

Tnere's always time for one last cast. One last cast for the day as the sun dips down. One last cast before I need to go home and assume my responsibilities. One last cast for the season before I pack up my gear. My last casts usually come in the form of deals I make with myself: five more casts in a fan pattern in this particular spot and then, convinced there are no fish out there just waiting for me to drag my lure through their quadrant, I will go home. I often cheat. I swear I'm going to make one last cast and then I make another, then another, and only when I am disgusted by my weakness, or seriously worried about time, do I make my final cast and go home. Sometimes, however, these last casts are the ones that bring in the fish. It makes little logical sense, I know, but I am convinced that the fraction of casts that qualify as last casts relative to all my other casts of the day disproportionately yield more fish. Who knows, maybe I take more chances on those last casts: casting into areas I usually overlook or trying out a lure that I haven't used before. But no matter how many last casts you take, there is always one, definitive, last cast, and then you need to go home.

Part of being an effective activist is knowing when to quit . . . and when not to quit. Back when I was a community organizer in the Lower East Side, we were working on a campaign to save local gardens. Residents had created gardens in reclaimed rubble-strewn lots back in the days when New York City's infrastructure was crumbling, realtors were disinvesting from the neighborhood, and the property was worth next to nothing. Now that gentrification had made the Lower East Side a desirable place to live for the more well-to-do, these abandoned lots turned community gardens were being sold off by the city to developers. Working with the people who had created them, we held protests outside the gardens, we had sleep-ins inside the gardens, we even unleashed 10,000 crickets inside an amphitheater during a land auction to halt the sales. (You really can get anything on the internet these days.) Yet despite our efforts, garden after garden was sold off and the gardeners were thrown off their lots. We were all getting dispirited and we seriously contemplated ending our campaign. But we staged one last action. We took over the central avenue in the East Village in the middle of the day, blocked traffic, fired up a mobile sound system, brought out planter boxes, planted flowers in the middle of the street, and held a raucous garden party that made all the local news channels. This action, planned in conjunction with other city-wide protests, was enough to convince a celebrity to donate a small fortune to buy the gardens for public use and push the city into selling them to her for a pittance. Did our one last protest save the gardens? No, but without it the gardens probably would not have been saved. Subsequently, the campaign became a matter of permits and legal wrangling, better left to lawyers and non-profits, and we knew it was time for us to pack up and go home.

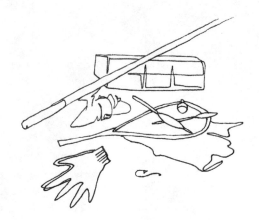

Packing Up for the Season

It's the week before Christmas, I'm up in Cape Cod, and this morning I go fishing in one of the nearby ponds the Massachusetts Department of Fish and Game website promised had been stocked with trout. The temperature dropped during the night and as I get up the ground is crinkly white with frost. I put on a lot of layers, topped with an old Irish fisherman's sweater that is usually too warm to wear, wind a scarf around my neck and pull on a wool cap, and go out to the shed to grab my gear. I park my aged Jeep by the roadside pullout as the sun is just coming up, walk the quarter mile through the woods to the water's edge, kick off my boots, pull on my waders, and walk out into the pond. And freeze. And catch no fish. And freeze some more. And still no fish. If this were an isolated incident, I might be tempted to go out again tomorrow, but over these past few weeks the days have been getting shorter, the weather getting colder, and I've been steadily catching less fish. Instead, I think I'll spend tomorrow packing up my gear for the season. I'll rinse off my lures and rub a little oil on the hooks so they don't rust, wipe down my poles with mild soapy water, grease my reels and let out the drag so the springs can become unsprung, and finally organize my tackle boxes. I've already started making a list of lures I want to buy over the next few months and I've begun searching eBay for a new rod for my city pier fishing. I also plan on watching a lot of fishing videos on YouTube this winter to teach myself how to fly fish properly. I'm already looking forward to spring.

My father was eighty-four years old when he died and for most of those years, he was an activist. His activism began in 1948 after he got out of the Army, went to college on the GI Bill, and became involved with a group of students protesting the then newly-formed Apartheid regime in South Africa. In the 1950s he registered Black voters in the Southern United States and in the '60s, as a young minister, he helped organize the second Selma march with Martin Luther King. In the 1970s he was a local secretary of the American Civil Liberties Union (whose work with the Black Panthers got the phones in my childhood home tapped), in the '80s he blockaded munitions trains carrying weapons headed to Central America, and in the '90s and into the new century he led interfaith peace protests in the small town in the Pacific Northwest where he retired. At his funeral, person after person stood up and testified to his inspiring example of a life of unceasing activism. But I knew the secret of my father's lifetime of commitment: he took breaks. Regularly. Growing up, I remember whole stretches of time when my father devoted himself to raising a family or working on his ministry or simply relaxing. As I grew into becoming an activist myself, I carried his lesson: breaks are as important as activity if you plan on being active for a long time.

It's Called Fishing, Not Catching

As an activist, you rarely win. You can work for months, even years, on a campaign and not see any result. Even when you win and a new policy is enacted, a fair contract signed, or there's a palpable shift in public opinion, it can all be undone in a moment and you have to start again. To remain an activist over the long haul, you have to learn to love the work itself. This means making the work lovable: activism should be about pleasure, play, and celebration more than the sacrifice, seriousness, and righteousness that too often characterizes the practice. Embracing the process also means acknowledging the long game. Yes, we must keep our eyes on the prize, and have faith that "the arc of the moral universe is long, but it bends toward justice," as MLK put it. But this also means recognizing how how long the arc stretches. One of the dubious advantages of becoming an activist in the US in the 1980s, when Ronald Reagan was a popular president, the Left was in shambles, and the Right was ascendant, is that I got used to not winning. Day in and day out, we marched and rallied, knocked on doors, and staged street theater performances, snatching a win here and there, but knowing full well the tide was against us. It was a time, as writer Rebecca Solnit put it, of "hope in the dark." It seems as if the tide is turning now. Reagan's popular conservatism has mutated into a rabid right-wing fanaticism attracting a dying demographic while the mainstream has moved decidedly left, with vibrant social movements on the ground and the moniker of "socialist" no longer conjuring up the bogeyman of totalitarianism (as much as the Right might try). It's a hopeful, productive time to be a progressive activist. But there will be other times, unproductive and dispiriting times, again. Indeed, as I do the final edits on this book, the US Supreme Court has overturned a woman's right to abortion. As with all things, there are seasons in activism, a time to win and a time to lose. Learning to love the *longue durée* of activism requires a certain detachment from the desired end. It's an exercise in what a philosophical friend of mine once called "existential activism," where you don't act to shape and change the world for any surety of result, but because to not act would mean ceasing to have a meaningful existence. Winning matters, and without wins social change doesn't happen, but it's the activity that makes winning possible. That's why it's called activism.

It's early spring, we have a new president, the pandemic has ebbed, and I am back in Cape Cod for a long weekend between classes to wake the house up from its seasonal slumber. I turn on the water, rake the leaves, survey the damage the winter has left, and make a to-do list. And, of course, I go fishing. Since the saltwater fish have not yet made their migration up the coast to the still frigid waters of New England, I head to my favorite kettle pond to fish for freshwater bass. I cast out and reel in. Nothing. I do it again, and again. Still no fish. I move around the pond and target some favorite spots: the submerged tree trunk, the branchy overhang, the "bass hole." I even abandon my beloved rubber worms and try out the new lures I bought over the winter. Not a bite. It's frustrating; I only have a couple of days to fish and here I am catching nothing. My only solace is knowing that I've had many such unproductive days before and will have many after. In order to catch a fish you have to spend a lot of time fishing, and a lot of that time fishing without catching. Of all the lessons I've learned fishing, it's this one I've found most valuable. To stay fishing, day after day, through good days and bad ones, you have to learn to love the process: the looking out over the water, strategizing the shoreline, psychologizing the fish, casting and retrieving, the waiting. With luck and skill, the process might yield a product and you'll catch a fish, but if you don't learn to love the process of fishing itself you might as well quit because the ratio between fishing and catching is mighty slim. As the hackneyed, but nonetheless true, adage goes: "It's called fishing, not catching."

Acknowledgments

The inspiration for this book came from two inspiring activist anglers. Nikola Pisarev, of the Contemporary Art Center in the Western Balkans nation of North Macedonia, who taught me through his personal example that fishing and activism have a lot to teach each other. And Micheal Young, from United for a Fair Economy in the United States, who encouraged me to make my musings on these lessons into a book. Tragically, Micheal died from cancer before this book was done. His last note to me included a picture of himself on a North Carolina beach with a forty-two-inch blacknose shark he had just caught cradled in his arms and a big smile on his face. It's how I will remember him. Elle Azul Duncombe-Mills deserves profuse thanks, and praise, for the beautiful drawings that grace each lesson. Working with her on these illustrations, and getting to know her as an artist and not only my niece, has been one of the great joys of creating this book. Friends, family, and colleagues read these lessons and offered helpful comments, including: Maz Ali, Reathel Bean, Matt Browne, Elizabeth Duncombe, Liza Featherstone, Warren Goldstein, Jennifer Bertolini Hallowell, Sarah Hill, and Mark Read. Special thanks to Phineas Baxandall, who talked me through many of these lessons on our morning beach runs, and my wife and unofficial editor, Jean Railla. Finally, I'd like to thank my official editor, Colin Robinson. Over twenty-five years and through three presses, Colin has steadfastly supported my odd ideas about culture and politics and has always sharpened my thinking about their alliance. I look forward to our next quarter century of collaboration.